Lisa Marie Bopp

Awesome Facts for Potter Fans

The Unofficial Collection

The Encyclopedia of
Secret Knowledge about the
Most Famous Wizard

© 2022 Nucleo
2. Edition

Author:
Lisa Marie Bopp

Translated by:
Kimberly Schnur

Inner illustrations:
Ninchik/Shutterstock

Published by:
Nucleo – a label of
MY DNA MEDIA UG
Ohmstr. 53
60486 Frankfurt am Main
Germany

ISBN:
978-3-98561-021-1

"Draco dormiens nunquam titillandus" is the Hogwarts School of Witchcraft and Wizardry slogan.

Translated, it means, "Never tickle a sleeping dragon."

A Proper Name

J. K. Rowling is one of the most famous authors in the world. However, some may not know that Rowling does not have a middle name. The "K." is for her grandmother, Kathleen. The initials appear on the book covers because her publisher feared a fantasy book about a male wizard wouldn't sell well if people knew it was written by a female author. Therefore, he insisted that Rowling use her initials instead of her full name. The problem then was that the name "J. Rowling" wasn't exciting enough, so she added the "K." for Kathleen.

The Magic Newspaper

The world of wizards in the *Harry Potter* movies was created with great effort. Every detail had to be perfect – even the individual pages and articles of the *Daily Prophet* or the *Quibbler*. Over 40 issues of the *Daily Prophet* were brought to life by the graphics department, and over 25,000 pages of the *Quibbler* were printed. Every article is unique; even advertisements and horoscopes found their place inside the newspapers. References to actors were often hidden in the texts for the crew's entertainment.

Rowling Does Not Know Harry Potter

J. K. Rowling is known for interacting with her fans. She answers questions and even participates in lively discussions concerning *Harry Potter*. However, even she gets in trouble sometimes. When Rowling tried to join a conversation anonymously in a chatroom called *MuggleNet*, she was told to be quiet because she did not know enough about the books.

Just Like Ron Weasley Would Do It

The third Potter movie, *Harry Potter and the Prisoner of Azkaban*, was no longer directed by Christopher Columbus. Instead, Alfonso Cuarón took his place. This change brought new challenges for the actors. Cuarón asked the young wizards to write an essay about their movie characters. Emma Watson – always the model student – wrote sixteen storming pages about Hermione. Daniel Radcliffe made it to one page about Harry. Only Rupert Grint did not write a single word about Ron. Well, his movie character would probably have done the same.

Short & Sweet

In his first movie, Harry Potter doesn't cast a single functioning spell with his wand.

Professor Dumbledore not knowing Harry Potter? Yes, that's possible. Michael Gambon, the actor who has played the headmaster since the third movie, had not read a single *Harry Potter* book before accepting the part. On set, he relied only on the script.

If J. K. Rowling taught at the Hogwarts School of Witchcraft and Wizardry, she would love to be a professor in charms. As an alternative, she would also be content with employment as an author of spells.

Despite being the longest book (768 pages), the fifth *Potter* book (*Harry Potter and the Order of the Phoenix*) has the shortest movie adaptation of the series. It only counts 138 minutes.

Snowball Battle with the Dark Lord

Lord Voldemort is considered the most dangerous wizard in the *Harry Potter* universe. Of course, that's no reason for Fred and George Weasley to spare him from a good old snowball fight. The jokers were only trying to hit Professor Quirrel with the bewitched snowballs. They succeeded, unaware that the Dark Lord was hiding under Quirrel's turban, on the back of his head.

Tiny Lice, Significant Impact

If only you could get rid of them by magic. In the magical world, you probably can, but things look a bit different in the real world. The little animals called lice can even bring a whole film set to a halt. That was the case when the crew tried filming *Harry Potter and the Chamber of Secrets*, the second *Harry Potter* movie. The shooting had to be stopped due to a lice outbreak among the many young actors.

A Stone with Many Names

Even though the US and Great Britain are both English-speaking countries, they have differences in naming things. For example, *Harry Potter and the Philosopher's Stone*, as the first book is called in the UK, was changed to *Harry Potter and the Sorcerer's Stone* for the American market. Those responsible thought the new name better fit the American audience. This change affected not only the books but also the movies. Several scenes had to be filmed twice – one take for the British and one for the American version.

Alohomora!

The door to the Chamber of Secrets is not opened that easily. A simple spell like the unlocking charm doesn't work on that particular kind of door. You need to speak Parseltongue to open it. The door itself then works mechanically. In the movie, not a single animation is required. You can even check out how that impressive work looks in real life when visiting the *Warner Bros. Studio Tour* near London. The big door regularly opens there – without the need of Parseltongue.

Wrong Pronunciation

Lord Voldemort is a name rarely spoken in the *Harry Potter* universe. Maybe it's not just because he's called "He-who-must-not-be-named" but because most wizards don't even know how to pronounce his name correctly. The name "Voldemort" has a French origin, and the "t" at the end is silent. The name even has a meaning. Loosely translated, it means something like "flight of death."

Not Enough Research

Snowy owls are primarily active during the day and are – especially the females – very quiet. J. K. Rowling obviously got to know of that too late when writing the second *Potter* book, *Harry Potter and the Chamber of Secrets*. At that point, Harry's pet owl had already showed her "special character" by her nightly adventures and blaming shouts directed at Harry. Maybe that's because Hedwig isn't just an ordinary snowy owl but a magical one.

Accio, Props!

When a great movie or series comes to an end, many props are left. But what exactly happens to all those things? Sure thing, the actors take them as souvenirs to always remember their time on set. Daniel Radcliffe, therefore, took not only the first but also the last glasses Harry Potter ever wore. Rupert Grint can now steal the light in his home with the Deluminator he took from the set. Furthermore, he took home a second prop: the sign of Privet Drive, number four. The one seemingly not wanting to quit being a witch was Emma Watson. She now claims as her own a wand, a Hogwarts cape, and a time-turner. Rupert Grint could have used the latter when he tried to steal a golden dragon egg from the set of *Harry Potter and the Goblet of Fire*. He was caught then and had to give it back.

The Hogwarts Dinosaur

Every now and then, a new name comes up that was inspired by the magical world of *Harry Potter*. Mostly, that is the case with naming newly discovered animals. But the long-forgotten ones can benefit from that kind of process, too. "Dracorex hogwartsia," a dinosaur, has been called the "Dragonking of Hogwarts" because of that.

Short & Sweet

The line "I didn't know you could read" was improvised by Draco actor Tom Felton. The line can be heard in *Harry Potter and the Chamber of Secrets* when Harry wears his glasses despite being turned into Malfoy's crony, Goyle. When Draco asks about the glasses, "Goyle" responds that he uses them to read.

Harry Potter significantly impacted J. K. Rowling's life. Before the books, the writer and billionaire relied on supplementary benefits.

It's no coincidence the Weasley family has a Ford Anglia as a magical flying car. A former schoolmate of Rowling had such a car – but without the flying mechanism.

Short & Sweet

Rowling invented the game Quidditch after she fought with her boyfriend. No wonder the game is such a violent one.

The Great Hall of Hogwarts is big enough to hold twenty-two double-decker busses.

When J. K. Rowling announced the death of two important characters in the last *Potter* book, she had to deal with the accusation of being a sadist.

According to the British retailer *Lost Universe*, Birmingham houses the most Slytherins. This claim results from a sentiment analysis counting the purchase of all Hogwarts-house-related merchandise in several British cities.

Potter Peanuts

Warner Bros. just needed to pay about two million dollars to get the movie rights. Today, this price would be far higher. Only the first book about the young wizard had been published in the US at the time of the purchase and only a few people knew about Harry and his adventure. So the price for the rights to get it on the big screen was relatively low then.

Early Departure

Some actors of the *Harry Potter* movies would have loved to leave the set earlier. Daniel Radcliffe wanted to quit his role as Harry after the third movie. He feared that he would only ever be identified as Harry Potter, making it hard for him to get other parts in the future. Later, he stated that he was fortunate to get the role and would continue to play the young wizard. His colleague Emma Watson considered quitting after the fifth movie because of her education. She was scared that the work on set would affect her time at Brown University. *Warner Bros.* later offered her a deal that made it possible for her to attend the university and stand in front of the camera.

Gone with the Wind

The Weasley family's house, also known as "The Burrow," is depicted as a very comfortable and cozy home in the movies and maybe a little chaotic, too. With such a big family, that isn't unusual. What is truly remarkable is the fact that the whole house seems kind of crooked. The set constructors did that on purpose and removed several beams or shifted a few walls. The house should get a unique look fitting the family living there. Well, mission accomplished.

Magical Age

The magic of *Harry Potter* enchants people all over the world. That his magic also seems to affect the age of the actor playing the young wizard is relatively unknown. Whereas book-Harry was born on July 31, 1980, actor Daniel Radcliffe did not come into this world until July 23, 1989. The actor, therefore, is nine full years younger than his movie self. An even more significant age gap can be spotted when looking at Moaning Myrtle and her actor. The 14-year-old ghost was played by a 36-year-old actress.

Haley-Harry

Daniel Radcliffe was almost not who we see as Harry Potter. At first, Haley Joel Osment was rumored to get the role before Daniel Radcliffe showed up. Osment was known for his role as the young medium in *The Sixth Sense*. Daniel Radcliffe won the race in the last moments as one of nearly 3,000 participants.

Devotion to the Job

The film crew on the *Harry Potter and the Chamber of Secrets* set must have loved the job. They didn't shy away from climbing into the London sewerage to find inspiration for the environment of the Chamber of Secrets. The adventure was worth it.

The Portraits in Hogwarts

The walls of Hogwart's staircase are decorated with numerous colorful paintings depicting famous witches and wizards. In reality, several show the movies' crew members.

A Professor to Fall in Love With

Sir Kenneth Branagh plays the charming professor Gilderoy Lockhart in the second *Potter* movie. The actor would have almost been a different one: Hugh Grant. He was on the verge of accepting when he noticed it would interfere with his schedule for his part in the movie *Two Weeks Notice*. In the end, he had to decline the offer.

Peeves the Troublemaker

There is another spirit wandering Hogwarts halls in the books and the videogames of the *Harry Potter* franchise: Peeves, the poltergeist. He is always up to some kind of mischief and pranks – much to the chagrin of Argus Filch, caretaker of the Hogwarts School. The poltergeist has been completely deleted from the script in the movie version because he did not significantly impact the story. Comedian Rik Mayall even shot a few scenes as Peeves for *Harry Potter and the Sorcerer's Stone*. Eventually, the film crew changed their mind and deleted Peeves entirely from the script.

On behalf of a charity event, J. K. Rowling wrote a prologue to *Harry Potter*. It takes place three years before the birth of the young wizard and has been sold for about 28,000 dollars.

A Loan for Harry Potter

Without the loan from a friend, J. K. Rowling would have never been able to create the *Harry Potter* books. The former welfare recipient took a loan of about several thousand pounds to get back on track. The single mother used the money to pay for her living and was able to get started with the first *Potter* book because of that. Of course, she paid back her debt and rewarded her benefactor with a flat in the middle of Edinburgh. That present now is worth over 250,000 pounds.

Dancing Lessons on the Set

All the actors had to take special dance lessons on the *Harry Potter and the Goblet of Fire* set to train for the dancing scene at the Yule Ball – everyone except Daniel Radcliffe. He had so many scenes in the movie that he just didn't have any time left for the dancing lessons. While the others trained for about three weeks, Radcliffe only had four days to learn the proper steps. While dancing, he was only filmed from his hips to his head, never showing his feet. That way, his poor dance attempts did not affect the scene.

Short & Sweet

Despite Harry's snowy owl, Hedwig, being female, the owls playing her in the movies were all male. The reason is the feathers of the male and female owls look different. The females have more black patterns, whereas the males are more white-colored.

J. K. Rowling finished her work on the second *Harry Potter* book shortly after the release of the first one.

Fred is the older one of the Weasley twins.

The movie adaptation of *Harry Potter and the Deathly Hallows* holds a little Easter egg for those paying attention to detail. In the café scene, a poster can be seen in the background, advertising a play called *Equus*. The play is a real one starring Daniel Radcliffe and Richard Griffiths.

Short & Sweet

The little slip of paper showing Harry's name in *Harry Potter and the Goblet of Fire* was not written by Daniel Radcliffe himself. Allegedly, his writing wasn't legible enough.

J. K. Rowling loves details. For the family tree of the Blacks, she not only came up with about 70 names but also with the relationship between the family members.

Lupin actor David Thewlis initially tried to get the role for Professor Quirrel. In the third movie, he was cast for the part of Remus Lupin instead.

More Fans Than Ever

Harry Potter and the Sorcerer's Stone reached about eight million dollars at the box office in China when first released. In 2020, things looked different. A special version of the movie in 3D and 4K optics fit for the Chinese market lured way more viewers in the cinemas. On the first weekend, the movie made a profit of 13.6 million dollars, almost doubling the numbers from the first release.

A Title without Explanation

Although the movie explained that Professor Severus Snape was the one behind the mysterious "Half-Blood Prince," the origin of the name was never revealed there. Book readers do have a head start concerning that question. In the books, it is explained that Snape's mother was a witch. On the other hand, his father was a muggle, making Snape a "Half-Blood." The "Prince" part of the title could be due to his mother's surname – Prince.

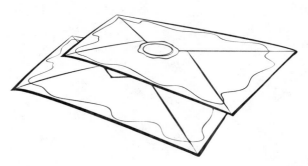

Talent Is Needed

In the fifth movie, *Harry Potter and the Order of the Phoenix*, many young wizards learn to cast the Patronus spell. One who is never shown casting that spell is Hagrid. For those wondering which form the magic would take on when released by the Keeper of Keys and Grounds of Hogwarts: It would have no form at all. According to J. K. Rowling herself, Hagrid cannot perform such a demanding spell.

Harry Potter and the Search for Names

Choosing the right name for every character in the book can be tricky. J. K. Rowling seems to have had trouble with that, too. Several character names were initially different. Hermione Granger was first called Hermione Puckle, and Draco Malfoy was almost known as Draco Spinks. Even Luna Lovegood and the Patil sisters, Padma and Parvati, were originally on the class list as Lily Moon and Madhari and Mati Patel.

Truly Bad

Lord Voldemort is the main villain in the *Harry Potter* series. Or isn't he? One person is even more feared than the Dark Lord: Dolores Umbridge. She is the most fearsome character in the whole story. Horror author Stephen King claimed the pink-clad woman is one of the creepiest film characters of all time. Only Hannibal Lecter would rival her psychopathic demeanor.

Owls Are No Pets!

One of the most loved characters in the *Harry Potter* world is Hedwig, Harry's snowy owl. The feathered hero was so famous that fans even considered buying an owl to keep as a pet. Of course, that is not animal friendly at all, so J. K. Rowling urged them to abandon that idea.

Hidden Details

Some movies include jokes during the credits. A small detail was included in *Harry Potter and the Sorcerer's Stone*: Voldemort's role isn't titled as such but called "He Who Must Not Be Named."

The Price of Youth

Working with young actors takes its toll. Snape actor Alan Rickman learned that first hand when Rupert Grint and Matthew Lewis stained his car with milkshakes while filming the fourth *Potter* movie. Why the two young actors were even in his car is unknown. When Rickman showed up with a new car on set, he ensured the two troublemakers would never come near his car again.

The "Stars" of the Magical World

The Black family appears to like astronomy very much. Many family members own the names of astronomical objects such as star constellations. By the fifth movie, names like Sirius, Cygnus, Arcturus, Pollux, and Cassiopeia appear on the family tree.

Short & Sweet

The choice of Adrian Rawlins for the part of James Potter must have been fate. The actor shares his birthday with his movie character: March 27.

Rowling wrote the first version of the Battle of Hogwarts very early and then put it into a safe. Back then, she didn't like the idea.

In 2010, J. K. Rowling reached the top of the list naming the UK's most influential women. Even Queen Elizabeth had to queue up behind the author.

The *Harry Potter* fanbase is significant. And it has quite the influence. Since the fifth novel, fans have even voted for the book covers in Germany.

Lucky Number Seven

The magical number seven is mentioned quite a lot throughout the *Harry Potter* series. There are seven books about seven school years and the destruction of seven Horcruxes. There are seven Weasley kids to count. Seven players make a Quidditch team. Hogwarts consists of seven floors and teaches seven core subjects. The number is mentioned several more times at minor occasions and big events alike.

Giant Wands

It's no wonder *Potter* fans might have felt the need to celebrate their passion for magic in a special kind of way in 2021. The year marks the 20th anniversary of the wizard's first movie adaptation. Maybe a good way to celebrate would be to pass through a walkway consisting of giant wands. People did have the chance for such a magical experience. An installation in Leicester Square, London, made it possible by showing off fifteen-foot-tall wands forming a 60-foot walkway. The wands were exact replicas of those in the *Harry Potter* and *Fantastic Beasts* movies.

Trouble in Paradise

Everyone knows the scene in *Harry Potter and the Prisoner of Azkaban* where Hermione hits the bullseye of Draco Malfoy's face. It leaves viewers wondering: Is that a real hit or just excellent acting? Looks like there really is a backstory. Emma Watson had a crush on Tom Felton. Felton made it clear that he only saw her as a little sister. A relatively short love story resulted in a satisfying clip for both the viewers and Watson herself.

Hogwarts Up Close

The world of *Harry Potter* is incredibly detailed. To ensure that all of these details were celebrated and contradictions were avoided, production designer Stuart Craig asked J. K. Rowling for her help. She was asked to explain the geography of Hogwarts so that the school and its environment could be shown in the best way. Rowling then drew a map on a DIN A4 sheet of paper. This map showed the Quidditch pitch, the Great Lake at which the castle was located, and the positions of important landmarks such as the Whomping Willow, Hagrid's hut, and the Forbidden Forest. The sketch was so detailed that it was still used as a reference years later.

Short & Sweet

In many movies, Easter eggs are hidden in certain scenes. Looking closely at the people roaming the Quidditch World Cup campground in *Harry Potter and the Goblet of Fire*, one can spot the house-elves Dobby and Winky riding by.

Even before the Deathly Hallows are mentioned in the movies, one can spot their symbol in *Harry Potter and the Goblet of Fire*. It hides in Dumbledore's office.

Not even the number of inhabitants of Germany, Italy and France added together can match the number of copies sold of the *Potter* books.

J. K. Rowling is the only author who became a billionaire with her bookselling only.

For Adults Only

Potter, the trouble-maker, made quite a mess when his first movie, *Harry Potter and the Sorcerer's Stone*, came out in Germany. Many children watching the film in the late evening hours were so excited that it resulted in many complaints. The kids could not calm down and started a ruckus. There were many calls for silence, so the cinemas enacted a ban for children to watch the late-night show of the movie. Tickets then would only be sold to adults. The only exception was when children were accompanied by their parents.

Delivery from Above

While pigeons are known for delivering letters, owls doing the trick can only be seen in the *Harry Potter* universe. Maybe it's because of the long training time the owls need to perform such a stunt. For the movies, they were trained over several months. However, the crew occasionally resorted to another method. They tied the packages or letters to the owls' feet and loosened the knot right over the dropping spot.

Short & Sweet

A wand made with a dragon heartstring is said to turn to the Dark Arts faster than any other wand. It is no wonder Lucius Malfoy's wand contains that core element.

Professor Dumbledore's full name is Albus Percival Wulfric Brian Dumbledore.

The Quidditch match Harry watched in his fourth adventure was the 422nd World Cup final. Ireland won the game against the Bulgarian National Team, 170–160.

The Hogwarts Express leaves King's Cross Station at Platform 9 ¾ every year on September 1 at 11:00.

Harry Potter as a Threat to His Readers

According to a pastor and teacher who spoke to several exorcists in the US and Rome, the spells used in the *Harry Potter* books are real and can evoke evil spirits. This statement resulted in St. Edward Catholic School in Nashville banning the *Harry Potter* books from the school library.

No Singing!

Imagine a singing Harry Potter or a dancing Draco Malfoy. If that thought makes you uncomfortable, you have something in common with J. K. Rowling. When the idea arose to create a musical based on the *Harry Potter* books, Michael Jackson offered to compose the music for it. However, Rowling wasn't keen on putting Potter on the big music stage, so the idea was quickly rejected.

Hidden Message

When the viewers first meet Professor Snape, he seems to be a very mean and strict teacher. The first question he asks Harry is what he would get if he added a powdered root of asphodel to an infusion of wormwood. That question has a hidden meaning when one knows the Victorian Language of Flowers. Knowing that asphodel is a special kind of lily and stands for "my regrets will follow you to the grave" and that wormwood means "absence" and is often associated with bitter sorrow, Snape seems to be trying to say, "I bitterly regret Lily's death."

Saved by an Eight-Year-Old

The *Harry Potter* books may have never been published had it not been for an eight-year-old girl. J. K. Rowling offered her manuscript of the first book to several publishers without success. At last, the manuscript landed in the hands of Nigel Newton of *Bloomsbury Publishing*. He didn't read it himself but gave it to his eight-year-old daughter, Alice. Because the young girl was so amazed by it and pestered him to get the whole story for her, he finally recognized its value.

Short & Sweet

To decide which character owned which skills or what each character wasn't good at took J. K. Rowling about five whole years.

In 2019, a first edition copy of *Harry Potter and the Sorcerer's Stone* was sold for about 70,000 pounds.

Have you ever met a "Harryplax severus"? This is the name of a kind of crab discovered a few years ago.
The name was (obviously) inspired by *Harry Potter* characters.

In the *Harry Potter and the Prisoner of Azkaban* movie, a statue at a fountain shows an eagle eating a snake. It is an allusion to the Mexican flag. Director Alfonso Cuarón – Mexican himself – wanted to place an artifact of Mexican culture into the movie.

The Language of Snakes

Parseltongue is a language in *Harry Potter* that allows speakers to communicate with snakes. The language itself, however, is real – kind of. Francis Nolan, a professor of linguistics at Cambridge University, developed the language specifically used in the *Harry Potter* movies. Nolan only defined a few rules and phonemes of the language of snakes, but these were essential for the actors on set. Without Nolan's work, they would not have known how to make the language come to life on screen.

Lost at Hogwarts

Only those paying attention to every little detail may have noticed: The rooms at Hogwarts sometimes shift. That's not because of the castle's quirks, like stairs changing their direction or paintings starting to move. No, it is simply because J. K. Rowling is merely human. She admitted she sometimes used the wrong geographic direction when describing a specific spot. It is hard to memorize every little thing about Hogwarts and its many rooms.

Talented on Many Levels

Evanna Lynch, the actor playing Luna Lovegood, has a second passion: making jewelry. The young woman even wears her creations in the movies. In *Harry Potter and the Order of the Phoenix*, she wears earrings that look like radishes. The bracelet she wears at the party at Slug Club in *Harry Potter and the Half-Blood Prince* is also made by her.

The Origin of a Werewolf

When Harry first met Remus Lupin, the professor already suffered from being a werewolf. That was not always the case: Lupin was bitten by Fenrir Greyback, a werewolf and Death Eater, when he was a little kid. Because of him, Lupin has suffered from lycanthropy since then.

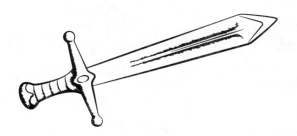

A Trick of Light or Simply Magic?

A true Potter fan may have noticed: Harry's eye color in the movies seems to change sometimes. In the books, it's clear as day. Harry Potter has green eyes. Actor Daniel Radcliffe, on the other hand, has blue eyes. A simple way to solve the problem: contact lenses. At least sometimes. Radcliffe didn't feel comfortable wearing them and had to take them out several times during the filming. Because of that, the crew decided to do it without the lenses after shooting one scene. That results in Harry having blue eyes in most scenes of the film – except from the very last one. At the parting at Hogsmeade Station, Harry has green eyes thanks to the contact lenses.

Asking Too Much

The teacher for Broom Flight lessons, Madame Hooch, is mentioned quite often in the books. In the movies, not so much. While viewers can see her in the first movie, *Harry Potter and the Sorcerer's Stone*, the other sequels have to do without her. Why? The actress Zoë Wanamaker simply charged too much. *Warner Bros.* then decided to cut her out of the script.

One of the first fan letters Rowling received for her books started with "Dear Sir," implying she was a man.

Hagrid 2.0

The Keeper of Keys and Grounds of Hogwarts is known to be one big-hearted giant. Only one person comes to mind when thinking of him: Robbie Coltrane. The actor seems to be the perfect candidate, but another actor could also have been chosen. Robin Williams was almost selected to play the part. Indeed, that wouldn't have been a bad decision either, but there is only one true Hagrid as of today.

Dark Humor

In *Harry Potter and the Chamber of Secrets*, the readers and main characters learn a lot about Voldemort's past. One of the things they learn is that Tom Riddle won an award during his stay at Hogwarts. Ron then jokes that the award was probably a prize for killing Moaning Myrtle. Later, it is revealed that Tom really had a part in her killing.

Apparent Resemblance

What started as a joke soon became a matter of international concern. A Russian newspaper reported lawyers of President Vladimir Putin wanted to sue *Warner Bros.* Why? Dobby the house-elf simply resembled the president greatly. The original article was only meant as satire, but international media and newspapers got that wrong and spread the word. Much later, the whole thing became known as a misunderstanding.

Cold as Ice

That Florean Fortescue, owner of the ice-cream shop at Diagon Alley, was abducted and later killed by Death Eaters is a fact only briefly mentioned in *Harry Potter and the Half-Blood Prince*. That detail should have had a much more profound impact on the story. It would have helped Harry with the search for the Ravenclaw diadem. Rowling made sure to mention Fortescue's knowledge of medieval magic when Harry first met him in *Harry Potter and the Prisoner of Azkaban*. He would have known a lot about the Elder Wand or the lost diadem. Sadly, this knowledge never made it into the story.

Short & Sweet

The actors playing the Weasley twins have brown hair in real life.

The spell on Hermione's magic bag that allows it to hold an unimaginable number of items also makes those items lighter.

Rowling wrote the first version of *Harry Potter and the Sorcerer's Stone* on a typewriter.

The search for the Deathly Hallows seems to take a while. In *Harry Potter and the Deathly Hallows – Part 1*, viewers can see the time difference when looking at Hermione's hair. While it is shoulder-length at the quest's beginning, it is much longer toward the movie's end.

Happy Death Day!

Harry's adventure mainly takes place in the '90s. That can be calculated in the second book, *Harry Potter and the Chamber of Secrets*. Harry and his friends are invited to a special kind of party celebrating the 500th death day of Nicholas de Mimsy-Porpington, who is better known as Nearly Headless Nick. He died in 1492, making the year of his 500th death day 1992, right in the middle of Harry's school time.

Just a Coincidence?

In 1998, the first *Harry Potter* book got published in the US. In the same year, the Battle of Hogwarts took place. Coincidence? When asked about that fact, Rowling only commented with "I open at the close." The same sentence is written on the Golden Snitch in which Harry finds the Resurrection Stone. If that isn't a hint...

The Relationship

It took seven books or eight movies for Hermione Granger and Ron Weasley to become a couple. More than a few fans had wished for a different pairing. Even J. K. Rowling herself wouldn't put Hermione and Ron together again. She admitted to regretting the decision somewhat.

Voldemort's Past

Voldemort is evil. But why, though? Can someone that heartless and without any understanding of love really exist? Yes, he can. The Dark Lord's past explains how he came to be that way. Tom Riddle's father was a muggle whom Tom's mother, Merope Gaunt, forced into the relationship using a love potion. However, a child fathered under the influence of a love potion can never gain the ability to love someone.

Sleeping Like a Potter

Would you like to sleep at the childhood home of Harry Potter? No problem. The centuries-old De Vere House can be booked for your next vacation on the *Airbnb* website. Several scenes of the *Potter* movies were filmed at this historic building and the surrounding town.

Every Day the Same

When thinking of Harry Potter, there's one thing that comes to mind: the famous scar, shaped like a lightning bolt. But Dumbledore, too, has a scar above his knee. It is shaped like a perfect map of the London Underground. Nevertheless, Harry's scar is far more famous. For the moviemakers, that comes with a lot of work. The scar had to be painted over 2,000 times. Counting not only Daniel Radcliffe, but his stunt doubles, too, it even had to be painted over 5,000 times.

Don't Forget!

Neville Longbottom is one of a kind, forgetting things regularly. Probably that's why his grandmother got him a Remembrall. Even though that little helper makes him remember whenever he forgets something again, it can't tell him what exactly it is he forgot. In the first movie, there is a scene at the Great Hall where Neville notices that he has forgotten something again. What that something might be never gets explained. If viewers pay attention, though, they can see everyone in the room wearing their cloak – except Neville.

Short & Sweet

The Hogwarts Express leaves London from King's Cross Station. While that station exists in London, the filming took place at the St. Pancreas station, which is 100 yards away. The film crew liked the front there better.

France is known for its unique translations of international terms. For example, the French call a Muggle a "Moldu," based on "mou du bulbe," which means something like "soft in the head."

To pass a certain subject at Hogwarts, the students have to take their O.W.L. exams. The letters stand for Ordinary Wizarding Level.

To Keep It Real

Hollywood stars like Tom Hanks, Leonardo DiCaprio, or Will Smith would never have been able to play a part in the *Harry Potter* movies. This is not by choice but because J. K. Rowling insisted on a British-actors-only crew on the set. However, a few exceptions were made: the Irishman, Richard Harris, playing Dumbledore in the first and second movie, and Madame Hooch actor Zoë Wanamaker, born in the US but is more famous in Britain.

Something Only Kids Would Love

Harry Potter could have stood in line with *E.T.* or the dinosaurs from *Jurassic Park*. Why? Because the *Potter* movies, too, were almost directed by Hollywood star Steven Spielberg. However, the famous director saw the young wizard's story differently and thought it would only be something children would enjoy. He wanted to combine several books to make animated movies but decided to refuse the offer.

Was It Worth the Trouble?

When a new *Harry Potter* book is on the verge of being released, several security measures ensure no information gets leaked before the official release date. Nevertheless, the Newspaper *Daily News* printed parts of the fifth *Potter* book, although it was off-limits at that time. Rowling sued the paper for 100 million dollars in compensation.

Harry Potter Protects the Rainforest

Harry Potter and the Order of the Phoenix was printed on 100% recycled paper in Canada. Author J. K. Rowling wanted her books to be published in an environmentally friendly way.

A Huge Demand

The band *Weird Sisters* performed on the Yule Ball in *Harry Potter and the Goblet of Fire*. The music group *Wyrd Sisters* took legal action, trying to prevent the movie's release in Canada because of the similarity of the band names. Their attempt failed.

Hogwarts Declining a New Student

When the letter from Hogwarts still takes its time coming, students think of new ways to find their way into the School of Witchcraft and Wizardry. Maybe there is a separate part of Hogwarts for university students? One candidate took his chance and wrote an application to Hogwarts University. He sent it to the UCAS – the Universities & Colleges Admissions Service. The employees there seemingly had a sense of humor because they wrote a letter, answering the request. Sadly, they had to decline the application because the available places would be scarce. After consulting their "Mystic-advisers," classes like "Wandology" would be highly in demand and hard to get into. The applicant would also need better grades in courses such as "Advanced Spellcrafting," "Mysticmatics," and "Shaft Design." Even his reportedly good grades in "Waving a stick about" and "Wearing a pointy hat" would not be enough to get a place at the university. He could, however, try again in the coming years by tying his application to an owl and hoping for the best.

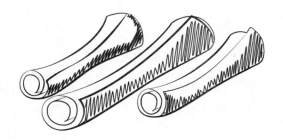

Short & Sweet

The name Harry Potter is mentioned more than 18,900 times in the books.

Daniel Radcliffe was sitting in the bathtub when he received the message that he got the role of Harry Potter.

To make the robbery scene at Gringott's in *Harry Potter and the Deathly Hallows – Part 2* look believable, more than 210,000 coins needed to be crafted.

The *Harry Potter* book series has sold over 500 million copies worldwide and was published in almost 80 languages. Amongst them were not only German and Italian but also ancient Greek, Latin, and other dialects.

The Queen's Handbag

A little movie, just about three minutes long, deals with the magical search for the Queen's handbag. The main characters – Harry Potter, Hermione Granger, and Ron Weasley – are played by the original actors from the *Harry Potter* movies. The movie was made to celebrate Queen Elizabeth II's 80th birthday.

Harry Potter on the Streets

How do magazines sold by homeless people and *Harry Potter* fit together? Looking at the sales figures in several German cities, they seem to fit quite well. The magazines were able to get the rights to print a few pages of *Harry Potter and the Order of the Phoenix* before the book was released officially. J. K. Rowling and the German publisher *Carlsen* provided the print rights for free to support the magazines.

A Witch's Teeth

In the books, Hermione Granger is a highly clever young witch with buckteeth. The film crew wanted her to have buckteeth in the movies to be as true to the original description as possible. Actress Emma Watson tried wearing the faux teeth, but she couldn't talk properly with them in. They had to cut them out of her costume.

Cloudy, with a Chance of Eyes Raining

Not pronouncing words clearly or having a strong accent can be fatal when working in the movie industry. But it is not just the actors who can cause problems with their pronunciation – directors may face the same difficulty. Alfonso Cuarón, the director of the third *Harry Potter* movie, learned this the hard way. The Mexican director wanted the train's windows to turn into ice when the dementors arrived at the Hogwarts Express. Unfortunately, the special effects crew thought he said "eyes" instead of "ice" and created a scene that featured falling eyes on the storyboard. Cuarón, confused at its look, cleared up the misunderstanding after that.

Harry's snowy owl Hedwig got her name from the sacred Hedwig, the patron of the sisters Hedwig.

These sisters were famous for committing themselves to the education of orphaned children.

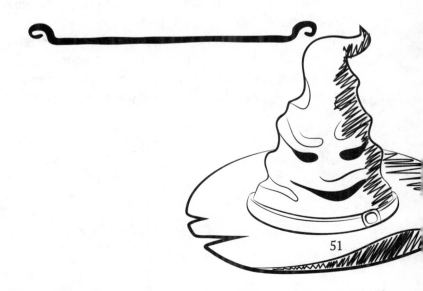

Pranks on the Set

Harry Potter actor Daniel Radcliffe liked a girl on the set. In one scene, which showed all the students together in the Great Hall with sleeping bags, he chose a place right beside the girl. He didn't expect actors Alan Rickman (a.k.a. Snape) and Michael Gambon (a.k.a. Dumbledore) to play a trick on him. With director Alfonso Cuarón's help, they hid a whoopee cushion in Radcliffe's sleeping bag. During filming, Gambon then used a remote control and earned a lot of laughs.

Spoiler Warning

For those who missed the Hogwarts Express and can't understand all the excitement coming with it, there now exists a perfect t-shirt. For *Potter* fans, on the other hand, the shirt may be hazardous. It reveals one of the most shocking events of the sixth *Potter* book. If you want to make fans really furious, this piece should be perfect: a shirt spoiling not only the death of Dumbledore but also the time it takes place. Written on the shirt is "Dumbledore dies on page 596 (I just saved you 4 hours and $30)."

The Servants of Death

J. K. Rowling seems to be a fan of deeper meanings. Therefore, the name of Voldemort's supporters is not only meant to sound intimidating but also has a meaning to it. The name "death eaters" arises from the term "beef eaters," referring to the lifeguards of the English king in ancient times. To fulfill their duty, they got more meat to eat than the rest of the people. In addition, the word "eater" in Old English can be translated to "servant."

When the Wizarding World Turns Into the Real World...

...even the dictionary gains new words. The names of different spells are not in the *Oxford Dictionary of English* yet, but the word that describes people without magic powers is. "Muggle" has been part of the reference book since 2003.

Short & Sweet

Six hours of make-up were needed to
transform Professor Lupin into a werewolf.

Harry Potter made J. K. Rowling richer than
the Queen of England.

Professor Slughorn's favorite food is
crystallized pineapple.

J. K. Rowling was awarded the Order of the
British Empire and an honorary doctorate
in literary studies.

Wand is translated to
"baguette magique" in French.

Werewolf Madness

Werewolves are naturally connected to the moon – the full moon, to be precise, makes them turn into scary beasts. In *Harry Potter*, the most famous werewolf is Remus Lupin, a professor at Hogwarts and a friend of Harry's father. His werewolf nature connects him to the moon, and his name has certain ties to it. Rearranging the letters of the name, one can read the words "primus lune." Translated, it means something like "the first moon."

A Little Secret

How was it possible for actor Alan Rickman to play his role of Severus Snape so convincingly? Even the first meeting between him and Harry has something mysterious to it. The potions professor not only was mean toward Harry but also looked at Harry in a special way. In the end, it was clear: Snape's intentions were never directed against Harry. Alan Rickman was able to play the part so well because he knew what Snape's past looked like from the start. J. K. Rowling initiated him into that secret.

Broken Promises

Nearly every trailer for the fifth *Potter* movie, *Harry Potter and the Order of the Phoenix*, included a line where Dumbledore warns Harry and tells him that he could never win against "him." The line never made it into the finished movie. Even the DVD versions of the movie didn't include that sentence.

The Not-So Floating Candles

Harry stumbles upon all kinds of curiosities in *Harry Potter and the Sorcerer's Stone*. Especially impressive: The Great Hall of Hogwarts is illuminated by numerous candles seemingly floating above the students' heads, thanks to magic. This posed a challenge for the movie crew. The candles were made using tubes filled with ethanol hanging from the ceiling with wire. In practice, this idea turned out to be a mistake. The flames caused the wires to melt, and the tubes fell on the tables. The candles ended up being computer animated without any fire hazards.

Harry Potter in Klagenfurt

Are you craving some butterbeer and a chocolate frog? The Austrian city Klagenfurt has solved this problem, thanks to Café Phoenix. It holds tons of books, magazines, and food and drinks, all in the style of *Harry Potter*. Candles float on the ceiling, and banners of the four Hogwarts houses decorate the walls. You can discover many details from the world of wizardry here.

Harry Potter and the Blacklist

The *Harry Potter* books made their way onto the most popular literature lists in the year 2000. They were also added to the list of the 100 titles that American adults don't want to see on the shelves of school and public libraries. *Harry Potter* ranked at place 48 on the so-called blacklist because many people believed that the book violated the principles of the Bible and religious morals.

Short & Sweet

Because many readers thought the first covers of the *Potter* books were too childish, the series got a special edition with new covers appealing to an older audience.

The day that Harry, Ron and Hermione fought a troll in the girls' bathroom in *Harry Potter and the Sorcerer's Stone* was when they all became friends (October 31, 1991). It is also the 10th anniversary of the death of Harry's parents.

Harry Potter and the Deathly Hallows was almost titled differently. Other titles in discussion were *Harry Potter and the Elder Wand* and *Harry Potter and the Peverell Quest*.

Homework at Magic School

Aside from charms, transfiguration, or arithmancy, students of Hogwarts had to take several other classes. Many actors were still young while filming the movies, so they had to do their real homework from their (muggle) school. The homework was integrated into the scenes of students doing their work for school. That way, the time on the set could be used more efficiently.

Enchanted Ice Cream

By now, there are countless recipes in the Muggle world for the butterbeer that is popular among Hogwarts students. However, ice cream of this flavor also exists. The manufacturer *Yuengling* has offered butterbeer ice cream since 2017. He added it to his assortment because of his children, who are big *Potter* fans. The ice cream mainly consists of buttercream and butterscotch.

Interesting Methods

Alfonso Cuarón took on the role of director in the third *Harry Potter* movie. He believed that children shouldn't be treated much differently than adults. This is also reflected in his peculiar methods while working with young actors. He gathers information about their interests to get the desired reaction and the perfect expression from the actors. He knew that Daniel Radcliffe had a weakness for actress Cameron Diaz, for example. Cuarón surprised the actor during one scene by saying that he should try to imagine Cameron Diaz in a thong. The perplexed expression that he got from Radcliffe in response was precisely what the director wanted for the scene.

Connected through the Stars

Harry Potter and his actor are connected. Although Harry's birthday is the 31st of July and Daniel Radcliffe's is the 23rd, they share a zodiac sign: Leo. There has to be magic at play here.

Drumsticks Are a Class of Their Own

Wands with the feather of a phoenix are some of the rarer magical items. Unfortunately, Daniel Radcliffe's wand was not magical. The actor broke over 80 wands because he often used them to drum on his knees during breaks.

A Dance for Two

The little dance that Harry and Hermione share in *Harry Potter and the Deathly Hallows* evokes a comforting feeling in many fans. It is an emotional moment between the two characters. The scene also served as a bit of a break after the fight with Ron and lifted spirits again. It never happened in the books, though.

Short & Sweet

Three gravestones with the names Thomas Riddle, William McGonagall and Elizabeth Moodie might have inspired J. K. Rowling. They can be found in the churchyard of Greyfriars Kirk in Edinburgh.

Wizards knew about the existence of another continent, North America, long before the Muggles found out about it.

Whereas Galleons, Sickles and Knuts are used for payment in the magical world of the UK, the magical currency in America is called the Dragot.

The Hogwarts School of Witchcraft and Wizardry is hidden somewhere in the middle of Scotland. The train ride from King's Cross takes around six hours. J. K. Rowling never explicitly mentioned the actual location in the novels.

Quidditch Ace

Professor McGonagall attended the Hogwarts School of Witchcraft and Wizardry in the early 1970s. As a grown-up, the witch teaches the subject of transfiguration. She could have chosen a different career path, though. A glorious future in the Quidditch field was ahead of her. After all, Hogwarts still had an award from 1971 on display that distinguished her as a Quidditch Ace.

An Anagram with Tradition

Every real Potter fan knows that "Tom Marvolo Riddle" is an anagram for "I am Lord Voldemort." But other names in the *Potter* universe also turn out to be anagrams: "Lavender Brown" can be reassembled into "Brand New Lover," subtly announcing Ron's first girlfriend through her name.

A Big Role Model

Oliveira Salazar reigned over Portugal from 1932 until 1968. The character Salazar Slytherin is inspired by the dictator. Rowling was very interested in Portugal's history while working in the country. She wanted to include her knowledge in the books.

Dumbledore Depiction Causes Trouble

It isn't news that movie adaptations often vary from the original books. Scenes are cut, dialogues are shortened, or background information is left out. But if changes are made seemingly without any reason behind them, fans can get angry. The depiction of Dumbledore in *Harry Potter and the Goblet of Fire* caused some fans to get upset, for example. After Harry's name came out of the Goblet of Fire, the headmaster was furious in the following scene. Panicking, he wants to know if Harry put his name in the goblet. He is rather relaxed in the books, though.

The bright witch
Hermione is the oldest
of the three friends in
the *Harry Potter* books,
whereas her actress,
Emma Watson, is the
youngest of the
wizard-trio.

Short & Sweet

The ghost that lives in the girls' bathroom of Hogwarts is most commonly referred to as "Moaning Myrtle." Her real name is Myrtle Elizabeth Warren.

Only one of the stairs in Hogwarts's giant staircase was real. The rest were added digitally in the movies.

Harry Potter and the Cursed Child sold over 850,000 copies during its first sales week in the United Kingdom. That makes it the fastest-selling theater script of all time.

Albus Dumbledore was 115 years old at the time of his death.

Patronus Couple

That Ron and Hermione are a good match is also reflected in their Patronus creatures. Ron's Jack Russel Terrier is known to chase otters. On the other hand, Hermione's Patronus, the otter, is related to the family of weasels, which can be associated with the Weasley family.

Change of Mind on Short Notice

Initially, only one movie was supposed to be released for each *Harry Potter* book. According to scriptwriter Steve Kloves, a movie for *Harry Potter and the Deathly Hallows* would have ended up running for four to five hours. That is why the last book was split into two movies.

Bookworm

Hermione's actress pointed out to the crew on the set of *Harry Potter and the Deathly Hallows* that there weren't enough books in Hermione's bedroom. The decorators followed this advice by adding more books.

Family Bond

Doesn't the young Tom Riddle in *Harry Potter and the Half-Blood Prince* have a striking resemblance to his older self, Lord Voldemort? A spell during the casting of the actor might be the reason. But the genes might have helped a lot more. The young Tom in the sixth movie is portrayed by Hero Fiennes-Tiffin, the nephew of Ralph Fiennes, who plays the part of the older Voldemort. The resemblance isn't a mere coincidence after all.

The Unlucky Number Thirteen

Divinations and omens play a significant role in the third part of the Potter series, *Harry Potter and the Prisoner of Azkaban*. Professor Trelawney, whose specialty is divination, refuses to sit down at a table with twelve people. The reason: Thirteen people at a table bring misfortune. Who first leaves the table dies. In the fifth movie, *Harry Potter and the Order of the Phoenix*, Sirius Black experiences this misfortune first hand. He is the first to get up from a table at which thirteen people are seated and loses his life in the same movie.

The Styling Secrets of a Dark Lord

Voldemort's actor, Ralph Fiennes, initially wore tights below his cloak. He couldn't correctly walk with them, though, because they kept slipping down. Eventually, he made the switch to socks. They were held up by garter straps to ensure they didn't slip either.

Colorful Cuisine

When seeing the festivals at Hogwarts in the movies, one's mouth might start to water. Tables are decked with mountains of tasty delicacies. But beware: Most of the food used on set was made with decorated synthetic resin. You should keep your hands off of that.

Dedication for Hamsters

Emma Watson kept a hamster as a pet. Of course, it couldn't be left by itself and was even allowed on set for *Harry Potter and the Sorcerer's Stone*, where it sadly died. The props department built a tiny coffin out of mahogany and velvet for its funeral – a magical gesture.

Enemies of the Past

The Battle of Hogwarts probably is the biggest fight Harry and his friends will ever face. However, in the past, they already faced several enemies. Among them were trolls, werewolves, and dementors. They meet all these creatures again at the big battle – but now the creatures are fighting for Voldemort. Good thing the Hogwarts students already know how to deal with them from previous encounters.

Little Hogwarts

Filming a whole castle can be a little tricky if the court doesn't exist in real life. As for Hogwarts, there were scenes taken in an actual castle, but there was also a replica of the magic school on a scale of 1:24. This model was mainly used for the spectacular tracking shots of the castle and its surroundings. The stunning replica can now be seen as part of the *Warner Bros. Studio Tour* near London.

Short & Sweet

The Latvian names of characters Hermione and Draco may hold a deeper meaning. „Hermiona Įkyrėlė" translates as "annoying"; the Latvian name „Drakas Smirdžius" means "smelly."

Hermione has a middle name: Jean.

In plagiarizing books, Harry Potter goes on adventures that are unknown to the rest of the world. The novel *Harry Potter and Leopard Walk Up to Dragon* was released in China, and *Harry Potter in Calcutta* is an Indian take on the series.

Harry's life in the Dursleys' home was anything but pleasant. To make the house and its interior seem incredibly uncomfortable, the production designer Stephanie McMillan only used furniture that she deemed very ugly.

Short & Sweet

Robbie Coltrane, the actor who played Hagrid, is one of fourteen actors that can be seen in every *Harry Potter* movie.

Severus Snape's name is mentioned over 1,800 times in the *Harry Potter* series.

The coronavirus pandemic affected the play *Harry Potter and the Cursed Child*. The play is usually split into two parts, but due to the pandemic, it was rewritten so that it could be shown in one piece.

The first *Harry Potter* movie, *Harry Potter and the Sorcerer's Stone*, initially had a running time of 170 minutes. However, 18 minutes ended up being cut.

The Torn Hat

The Sorting Hat usually knows who belongs in which Hogwarts house very quickly. But sometimes, it is torn between different possibilities. In some instances, the hat even takes over five minutes to ponder. Witches and wizards that keep the hat on its toes in such a manner are also referred to as "Hatstalls." Only two of them are ever mentioned in *Harry Potter*. Professor McGonagall almost ended up in Ravenclaw instead of Gryffindor. The Sorting Hat took over six minutes to decide. Peter Pettigrew also didn't get assigned immediately. Next to a Gryffindor, he might have been – who would've guessed – a Slytherin.

Tricks of Movie Making

One could say a man reaching six feet in height is pretty tall. However, it is a little too short for a half-giant like Rubeus Hagrid. According to the books, the Keeper of Keys and Grounds of Hogwarts makes it to storming eleven feet, six inches, so actor Robbie Coltrane had to use a few tricks to make him seem so tall. Hagrid's hut has two versions, for example. One makes the actor seem especially big; the other makes everyone else seem particularly small.

Great Emphasis on Animal Welfare

Owls, rats, snakes, and cats – all of these animals could be found on the sets of the *Harry Potter* movies. Next to the real-world animals, other creatures find their place in the *Potter* universe. Obviously, no creatures were supposed to be harmed by the shooting. It's good that the producers explicitly state in the credits of *Harry Potter and the Goblet of Fire* that no dragon was injured during filming.

The Show Must Go On

Actress Dame Maggie Smith, also known as Professor McGonagall, was battling breast cancer during the *Harry Potter and the Half-Blood Prince* shooting. With a wig and inspiring strength, she managed to get through the entire shooting and those for the next two movies. She wanted to be able to stay on the set for the *Harry Potter* series until the last shooting day and, according to her own words, "pull herself together a bit." She managed to do just that and won the fight against cancer.

Worried that an early release of *Harry Potter and the Prisoner of Azkaban* would cause students to skip school, the British publisher of the Potter series, *Bloomsbury*, asked bookstores not to sell the book before school was over.

Quodpot

Quidditch is a popular sport in the wizarding world. This only seems to apply to Europe, as Quodpot is preferred in the United States. The game is a take on American football, with teams of elven facing off. The team that manages to get the ball ("Quod") into the "pot" as fast as possible, wins. To make the whole thing a little more interesting, the ball explodes after a while. If a player is in possession of the ball and it blows up before landing in the pot, the player must sit out the rest of the game.

A Dangerous Job

Being a stuntman is a dangerous profession. While shooting *Harry Potter and the Deathly Hallows*, stuntman David Holmes hurt himself so badly that he ended up with paraplegia. Following the incident, Daniel Radcliffe raised money for him.

Old Acquaintances

It is not unusual for authors to find inspiration in their environments. With characters in particular, there are often parallels to real people. Professor Snape is based on a real personality: J. K. Rowling's past chemistry teacher was the basis for the initially mean-spirited Head of Slytherin. The feared Dolores Umbridge is supposedly also inspired by a real person from Rowling's life.

Paying Last Respects

In the fourth *Potter* book, one student starting at Hogwarts is based on a real-life person. Natalie McDonald is assigned to Gryffindor in *Harry Potter and the Goblet of Fire*. The story behind that name is that Natalie had leukemia, and her friends wrote a letter to J. K. Rowling pleading her to tell Natalie how *Harry Potter* continues. Rowling fulfilled this wish, but the girl died before the information arrived. To pay her the last respects, the student is named after her.

Short & Sweet

The Hogwarts acceptance letter is usually delivered by owls. If a future Hogwarts student has Muggle parents, a professor will visit the family and explain the circumstances instead.

There are 142 stairs in Hogwarts.

Hogwarts is so contorted and full of curiosities that, according to Dumbledore, no living or dead soul exists that knows all of the castle's secrets.

The first Triwizard Tournament only took place 300 years after Hogwarts was founded. The competition was meant to allow students of different European wizarding schools to interact.

Kiss on Command

It's not easy for every actor to show feelings convincingly on the big screen. Kissing is probably one of the leading disciplines, which is shown in the number of attempts. The actors of the *Harry Potter* movies also had their problems with it on set. The kiss between Ron and Hermione needed six takes; Ron and Lavender needed fifteen, and Harry and Ginny needed ten, but the kiss between Harry and Ginny took the cake with thirty attempts.

The Smuggler of Sweets

Children on set can only mean one thing: sweets on set. At least this assumption holds true for the young Tom Felton. The actor who played Draco Malfoy regularly smuggled sweets onto the *Harry Potter and the Prisoner of Azkaban* set. To do so unnoticed and get through the shooting, he hid the sweets in the pockets of his cloak. It soon became apparent, though, and the pockets were sewn shut because he repeatedly tried this trick.

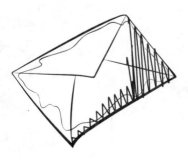

Script Drama

After a night spent drinking alcohol, one may forget about some things. These might be minor details, but they could also lead to bigger problems. That is precisely what happened in England in 2010. After a night out, something was left behind at the *Waterside Tavern*. The set crew of the *Harry Potter* movies frequented this pub and one night left behind the script for *Harry Potter and the Deathly Hallows*. The movies were still being shot at the time, meaning the script was supposed to be top secret. The person who found the forgotten script handed it over to a big news company, which reported on the incident. After that, it was returned to *Warner Bros.* None of the contents were leaked.

Short & Sweet

Over 770 characters appear in the
Harry Potter books.

The book *Culpeper's Complete Herbal:
Over 400 Herbs and Their Uses* served as a
reference for the numerous magical plants
in *Harry Potter*.

Harry encounters the bus conductor, Stan
Shunpike, and driver, Ernie Prang, during
his ride on the Knight Bus. Both are named
after Rowling's grandfathers.

Dumbledore in Norwegian isn't the same
as it is in English. His name is
"Humlesnurr" there – "Humle" meaning
bumblebee, and "Snurr" can be translated
to "to rotate."

Birds of a Feather Flock Together

While certainly not everything that happens in *Harry Potter* is based on J. K. Rowling's life, there are some similarities between her life and the narrative. None other than Hermione Granger is based on the author herself. Just like Hermione, Rowling was a bookworm in her childhood. It's no surprise, then, that Hermione's Patronus is an otter – J. K. Rowling's favorite animal.

High Praise

Getting praise from bestseller author and horror legend Stephen King is something extraordinary. *Harry Potter* author J. K. Rowling can pat herself on the back for that, as the famous writer loves the *Harry Potter* novels. He even compared them to other young adult novels: While *Harry Potter* deals with inner strength and doing your best in the face of injustice, the vampire saga *Twilight* is merely about a girl who thinks it is essential to have a boyfriend.

Train Rides for Wizards

Wizards, too, sometimes need to use trains. However, the use of additional platforms in the Muggle train stations would be too obvious. To enable the trains to operate between those of the Muggles, there needed to be platforms between them. This is why the wizard trains depart on fraction-numbered rails. Next to platform 9 ¾, there are numerous other magic rails. For example, a train similar to the Orient Express departs from platform 7 ½. It allows wizards to visit various European cities that are accessible only to witches and wizards. Some platforms are open only for specific purposes. For example, special trains depart on platforms for big events such as the Celestina Warbeck concert.

Author in Front of the Camera

J. K. Rowling almost contributed to *Harry Potter* in another way aside from being the author. She could have taken on the role of Lily Potter in the films. She didn't think she was a good actress and denied the offer.

Short & Sweet

The first printing of the first *Harry Potter* book produced approximately 500 copies. Over twelve million copies were produced for the final book.

Appropriate for their lives as jokers, the Weasley twins were born on the day of pranks: the 1st of April.

Daniel Radcliffe used around 160 pairs of the *Potter* glasses during filming. A Reparo spell might have been helpful.

Doves are one of the few fears that Harry Potter hasn't overcome.

Deadly Game

One of the many new things that Harry Potter learns during his first year at Hogwarts is Wizard's Chess. Harry and Ron play a game during Christmas time, and Harry's knight loses to Ron's queen. Later, they play again to find the Sorcerer's Stone. This time, they themselves are the pawns. During this match, Ron is the knight and loses to Queen Harry. The chess move from their first game repeats itself in reverse.

Nagini Is Real

Things don't always go as planned, especially when animals are on set. Oftentimes, they don't behave like they're supposed to. In such cases, they tend to be replaced by computer-animated versions. This was no different during the filming of *Harry Potter*. Even though a few special effects were animated, some real animals were on set. One of them was a python that embodied Voldemort's companion Nagini.

A Cold Treat

Rupert Grint, the actor who played Ron Weasley, wanted to become an ice cream man when he was younger. He fulfilled his childhood wish when he bought an ice cream truck with his acting salary. He then drove through nearby towns and gave out ice cream to children – for free, of course.

Steep Entrance

Hermione's actress Emma Watson made a big entrance during the Yule Ball in the movie *Harry Potter and the Goblet of Fire*, but she was so nervous that she ended up falling down the stairs on her first try.

Awkward Situation

Seeing yourself in video recordings is often a weird feeling. Do actors feel the same way when watching their own movies? At least, Daniel Radcliffe isn't a fan of seeing himself on the big screen. But there is one movie that he especially doesn't like watching: Radcliffe considers his acting in *Harry Potter and the Half-Blood Prince* as his weakest performance. Maybe this opinion is related to the fact that the actor had drinking problems during the movie's filming. He has overcome these problems since then.

No Stone Left Unturned

After the final battle in *Harry Potter and the Deathly Hallows – Part 2*, Hogwarts lies in ruins. Five trucks with a capacity of 32 tons were needed to transport the rubble on set. However, the load wasn't made up of real stone, as styrofoam was used instead.

A Slytherin Thief

Alan Rickman and Jason Isaacs seem to have taken their roles as villains too seriously. While Snape's actor Rickman only stole a few coins during the shoot in Gringotts Wizarding Bank, Lucius Malfoy's actor Isaacs had his eye on the copies of the *Daily Prophet*. Unlike his co-star, he asked director David Yates for permission beforehand (which was granted to him), but while he was leaving the set, a crew worker pointed out that props had to stay on site. Isaacs later described this incident as embarrassing – especially because he didn't get anything out of it.

Hedwig, Hedwig and Hedwig

We can see three different versions of Harry's owl in *Harry Potter and the Sorcerer's Stone*. This doesn't refer to the angle at which it was filmed but to the owl itself. Three different members of the species portrayed Hedwig. Their names were Gizmo, Ook and Sprout. Each owl had its own specialty for the needed scenes, but Gizmo had the most appearances.

Short & Sweet

The manuscript for *Harry Potter and the Sorcerer's Stone* was rejected by eight publishers before publishing company *Bloomsbury* gave it a chance.
This may have been the publisher's best decision ever.

The chair in which J. K. Rowling wrote the first two *Harry Potter* books was sold at an auction for 278,000 British pounds. It was signed by the author beforehand.

After J. K. Rowling finished the last *Harry Potter* book, she left a message in the hotel room where she had written the novel. On the back of a marble bust, she wrote that J. K. Rowling had finished *Harry Potter and the Deathly Hallows* in this room (552) on January 11, 2007.

Among Malfoy Men

Draco Malfoy is a spoiled child who threatens to speak to his father every time he gets into trouble. His father seems to follow his son's every request in the books. Loved and sheltered, Draco gets showered with magical gifts. The father–son relationship seems a lot tenser in the movies. Draco can seemingly never live up to his father's expectations.

Neat Handwriting Needed

The Pensieve is located in Dumbledore's office. He uses it to store countless memories in a cabinet so he can look at them again and again. The movie crew made its mission to make the glass bottles in which the memories are stored look as authentic as possible. Crew members labeled more than 800 bottles by hand.

Clear the Ring!

Fighting a snake can lead to some severe injuries. For instance, Harry Potter actor Daniel Radcliffe ended up with a black eye. No real snake was at play, though. The actor quarreled with a boxing glove attached to a stick. It was later turned into a snake in the movie.

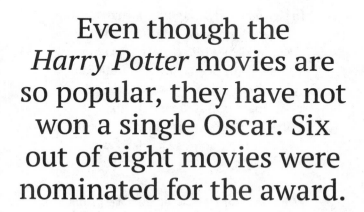

Even though the
Harry Potter movies are
so popular, they have not
won a single Oscar. Six
out of eight movies were
nominated for the award.

Short & Sweet

In German and Icelandic, journalist Rita
Skeeter's name was changed to Rita
Kimmkorn. While the original name
would've only been a little bit unfamiliar
in German, it would've caused roaring
laughter in Icelandic theaters.
The last name sounds similar to "skita,"
a vulgar paraphrase for defecation.

An honor for the soccer club *West Ham
United*: The London-based club found its
place in the *Harry Potter* books because
a childhood friend of J. K. Rowling
was a big fan.

The birthdays of the main characters are
the 31st of July (Harry),
the 19th of September (Hermione)
and the 1st of March (Ron).

Hard Shell, Soft Core

The most dangerous inmates of the US are in the high-security prison Guantanamo Bay. They seem to turn back into children when it comes to *Harry Potter*, though. The *Harry Potter* novels were the most asked for books in the prison's library. Some inmates would also like to watch the movies.

Clothes Make the Man

Dolores Umbridge gets more evil and hysterical as time goes by. In the movies, this is not only shown through her behavior but also her clothing. The school's temporary headmaster wears soft pink tones when she first appears. Little by little, her attire turns into a shrill and darker pink. The change in her behavior is subliminally emphasized through this change. Voldemort's clothing also gives some insight into his well-being. While his cloak is pitch black after his resurrection, it continues to fade until it almost turns grey. The reason for this is the destruction of the Horcruxes. The weaker he gets, the paler his clothing turns.

A Real Puppet Theater

The dementors were meant to appear scary and frightening in the movies – ideally without any computer animation. Much effort was put into them to achieve this. The dementors were reimagined as puppets and filmed underwater, capturing the feeling of the creepy flowing cloaks of the dark creatures. Unfortunately, the puppets were very hard to control underwater. However, the effort wasn't wasted. The water recordings later served as the base for the computer-animated soul suckers.

A Look at the Future

Many movies use foreshadowing. *Harry Potter and the Half-Blood Prince* isn't an exception. The memory in which viewers can see a young Tom Riddle inside his room in an orphanage for the first time gives a closer look at Voldemort's past and hints at the details of the Horcruxes. The camera zooms in on seven stones on the window sill and a picture of a cave on the wall. As viewers later learn, the cave is where Voldemort hides one of his Horcruxes. The seven stones also represent the number of the Dark Lord's Horcruxes.

Surveillance Similar to Azkaban

Security guards watching your every move. Searches when leaving the building. Highest secrecy level. One might think that this refers to Azkaban. But these were the circumstances of a printing company in Germany. The seventh and last book of *Harry Potter* was printed there – under strict conditions. To ensure that no employees leaked anything or even smuggled a book or a few pages outside, they had to sign a confidentiality declaration and undergo daily searches. A violation could lead to being fired. Employees were watched to ensure that nobody gained access to any information too early. The printers mainly worked in the dark so that no one could read the pages in passing.

Short & Sweet

The *Harry Potter* books value authenticity,
notwithstanding the magical aspects. Even
a real-life heatwave from summer 1995
made its way into the books.

Tom Riddle was born on December 31,
1926. He died during the final battle for
Hogwarts on May 2, 1998 – meaning he
was 71 years old at the time of his death.

J. K. Rowling's favorite chapter is
Chapter 34: "The Forest Again" in the
seventh *Potter* book, *Harry Potter and the
Deathly Hallows*.

In the Italian version of the *Potter* books,
Professor Dumbledore is called
Professor Silente.

A Difficult Decision

Arthur Weasley almost didn't survive the fifth *Harry Potter* novel. J. K. Rowling was thinking of killing the head of the Weasley family. However, she couldn't bear to kill the father of seven children. Later on, Sirius Black had to give his life to balance it out.

Polyjuice Potion Is Puzzling

Actors were playing other actors as they played other actors. Copying the peculiarities of another actor isn't an easy task. The Polyjuice Potion can lead to some confusion. This is the case in *Harry Potter and the Deathly Hallows – Part 2*. Hermione transforms into Bellatrix Lestrange to gain access to her vault in Gringotts Wizarding Bank. In „real life," Helena Bonham Carter (Bellatrix) had to pretend that Hermione, alias Emma Watson, was stuck in her character's body. Luckily, Emma Watson helped her co-star by playing a practice run of the scene herself. This way, Helena Bonham Carter could use it to guide her own performance.

A Double-Life in the Potter Universe

Eddie Redmayne became well known within the *Harry Potter* universe through his role as Newt Scamander in *Fantastic Beasts and Where to Find Them*, but he had previously auditioned for the part of the young Voldemort in *Harry Potter and the Chamber of Secrets*. He never got a callback.

Some Mistakes Are Hard to Remove

Sometimes, there are minor mistakes in movies that can be noticed in the final product. *Harry Potter and the Prisoner of Azkaban* is no exception. When Harry and Hermione start their quest to save Buckbeak using the time-turner, one can see the microphones on the backs of their shirts.

A Magic Trick Too?

The audience gets to know Lavender Brown more closely in the sixth *Harry Potter* movie as she is Ron's rather irritating first girlfriend. In this movie, she is played by Jessie Cave, a Caucasian actress. But Lavender already had a previous appearance in *Harry Potter and the Prisoner of Azkaban*, in which an actress with darker skin portrayed her.

Don't Fool around with Wands

On set, Neville's actor Matthew Lewis was hurt by Helena Bonham Carter, also known as Bellatrix Lestrange. She only wanted to threaten the poor Neville and keep him in check with her wand. But Lewis moving while she held the wand to his ear ended up hurting his eardrum. He only confessed to her how bad the injury really was a few days later.

Sweet Tooth

Getting paid for eating sweets – does it sound like the dream? Apparently, it was for Rupert Grint. According to co-actor Daniel Radcliffe, Ron's actor loved shooting takes of his first meeting with the characters of Hermione and Harry on the Hogwarts Express. No wonder – Ron's principal activity during that scene was eating sweets.

Jumped the Gun

It was good while it lasted: *Harry Potter and the Half-Blood Prince* was sold almost two weeks too early in Canada. A few lucky buyers were able to get their hands on copies before the mistake got noticed. Shortly after, lawyers intervened. A court order obligated the (un)lucky buyers to return the books and not speak about their contents. After the book's official launch, the affected people would receive a signed copy to make up for the mishap.

Short & Sweet

Gilderoy Lockhart owns a portrait of himself that shows him painting a picture of himself. You can see it in the professor's office during Harry's second school year.

The story of the Deathly Hallows is told in *The Tale of the Three Brothers*, part of Rowling's book *The Tales of Beedle the Bard*.

Ron's middle name is Bilius.

The initials Harry finds on the fake Horcrux, R. A. B., stand for Regulus Arcturus Black, Sirius's brother.

The number of spells in the *Harry Potter* novels multiplies. While only seven spells appear in *Harry Potter and the Sorcerer's Stone*, there are 128 in *Harry Potter and the Deathly Hallows*.

Dementors out of Depression

After her mother's death, author J. K. Rowling was looking for a way to express her sadness. The depression caused by this death led to the characterization of the dementors. The coldness, emptiness, and sucking of the soul associated with dementors reflect the author's feelings during this difficult time. The only cure: chocolate.

No Special Treatment for Dark Wizards

Even though Voldemort's death in the movies is theatrical as the character turns to dust in front of everyone, the death curse Avada Kedavra always has the same effect in the books. The person struck falls to the ground lifeless. Rowling wanted to emphasize that everyone is the same in death.

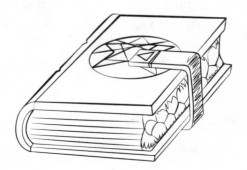

Spells From Armenia

The spells in the *Harry Potter* universe are often derived from Latin. This is shown in spells like "Wingardium Leviosa." But the three unforgivable curses were derived from the Old Armenian language. "Avada Kedavra" can be loosely translated to "I destroy as I speak." Fun fact: "Abracadabra" can be translated from Old Armenian as well and means something like "I create as I speak."

Childhood Memories

Pretty much everyone can relate: When you're younger, the other gender isn't exciting but simply annoying. It's even more embarrassing when you're supposed to hug them. Emma Watson seems to have felt the same when filming a scene for *Harry Potter and the Chamber of Secrets* where she hugs both male main characters. It was so embarrassing for the young actress that the scene was rewritten: Hermione was now only supposed to shake Ron's hand and give Harry a short hug. But this was still too much for the actress. She kept letting go of Daniel Radcliffe too early, which is why the scene was edited and frozen for a short time to make the hug seem longer than it was.

Short & Sweet

The movie set for the main street in Godric's Hollow is the same set that was used for Hogsmeade in *Harry Potter and the Prisoner of Azkaban*. Only a few adjustments were made.

The Trace is a charm that allows the Ministry of Magic to track whether underage wizards are using magic. Wizards only lose the Trace when they turn seventeen.

Despite the many fans of the *Harry Potter* franchise, the Catholic church seems to have a different opinion. Pope Benedict XVI deems the Potter novels un-Christian.

A tombstone with the name Harry Potter can be found in a graveyard in Tel Aviv. It belongs to a British soldier who died when he was only 19 years old.

The Real Hogwarts

Next to the replica of the castle, a real castle also served as the filming location for Hogwarts. The Alnwick Castle in Northumberland was used to shoot the inner court footage. The castle can be seen in *Harry Potter and the Sorcerer's Stone* and *Harry Potter and the Chamber of Secrets*. Harry's flying lessons also took place there.

A Furry Adventure

Animals can turn a movie set upside-down. The cat that played Mrs. Norris, caretaker Filch's pet, in *Harry Potter and the Sorcerer's Stone* kept the movie crew on edge for two whole days. It ran away while filming and only came back 48 hours later.

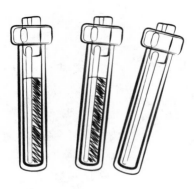

Paper for the Author

J. K. Rowling amassed mountains of loose papers. She didn't purchase them all herself, though; they were sent to her by worried fans. After the *Harry Potter* author complained about the city not having enough paper for her to write on, she was regularly showered with paper by fans.

Hermione's Tutoring

One of the brightest witches in Hogwarts, Hermione Granger, possessed a rather unusual name that led to a lot of confusion. An extra scene was added to *Harry Potter and the Goblet of Fire* in which Hermione mentioned and explained her name to Viktor Krum to end the confusion about its pronunciation once and for all.

Harry Potter and the Handsome One

The *Harry Potter* novels may be done, but the story continues without J. K. Rowling having to lift a finger. A robot wrote an additional chapter for the *Potter* books. The goal was to create automatic writing software. The developers fed the robot with *Harry Potter* novels to see whether it could use the information to write a text in the same style. The robot did indeed continue the story – but differently than expected. It created a chapter called *Harry Potter and the Handsome One* in which two Death Eaters kissed, Ron ate Hermione's family, and Harry fell down stairs – for several months.

Voldemort Times Six

The Dark Lord has numerous appearances in *Harry Potter*, whether as a young Tom Riddle, a teenager, or ultimately, the resurrected Lord Voldemort. Six different actors were needed to take on the character's role throughout the movies.

Keep Up Appearances

The actor who played Dudley, Harry Melling, lost a lot of weight during the years when the movies were filmed. He lost so much that he had to wear pads in *Harry Potter and the Deathly Hallows* to make up for it – even on his face! The makeup team worked on them for almost six months to make sure that they looked realistic in close-ups. Ultimately, most of his scenes had to be edited in post-production.

No More Fan-Hosted Potter Events

Potter fans are not allowed to host big events around their favorite franchise. *Warner Bros.* forbids festivals that use names, locations or items from the *Harry Potter* universe. The fan festival called *Harry Potter Festival* not only had to be renamed "Wizards & Wands," but some activities had to be canceled, such as "Defense Against the Dark Arts."

Short & Sweet

A little girl is responsible for Richard Harris taking on the role of Albus Dumbledore in the first two movies. The actor's then elven-year-old granddaughter Ella was a big fan of the *Harry Potter* novels. She threatened to never speak to her grandfather again if he refused the role.

The school year in Hogwarts always begins on the 1st of September.

Daniel Radcliffe not only had an allergic reaction to the green contact lenses he had to wear for the role of Harry but also to his glasses, which were then changed.

Many potions that were drunk by Harry and other wizards throughout the movies were actually soup. The carrot coriander soup was the actors' favorite.

Quality and Quantity

The props department's work on the set of *Harry Potter* is almost magical. Crew members turned wood, plastic, and rubber into more than 3,000 wands for the actors – with not one looking like the other. Each wand is unique and customized to fit the personality of its owner.

Backed Out at the Last Minute

Gone Girl actress Rosamund Pike was supposed to play *Daily Prophet* journalist Rita Skeeter. She had accepted the role but backed out when she learned that she would have only brief appearances after the fourth *Harry Potter* movie.

Special Delivery

Mail is usually delivered to Hogwarts by owls. A few letters wouldn't pose a problem for the feathered mailmen. In one of the movies, however, the owl wasn't strong enough to carry a broom. An exact paper copy of the flying broom, crafted by hand, was delivered to Harry by owl mail instead.

For fear of the audience recording *Harry Potter and the Half-Blood Prince*, some cinemas in German cities were monitored with night-vision devices.

Dementors in Reality

Dementors are horrifying creatures that serve as guards and punishment for the prisoners of Azkaban. They are especially feared because of their ability to suck out the souls of their victims. A similar creature exists in real life. A species of wasps uses neurotoxins to make victims obedient, similar to reomoving their souls. The species was fittingly named "Ampulex dementor."

Short & Sweet

The British wizarding community has its own currency, consisting of Galleon, Sickle, and Knut. One galleon is worth around five British pounds.

J. K. Rowling would've loved to have Terry Gilliam as the director of the *Harry Potter* movies. He is known as a co-founder of the group *Monty Python*. Her wish was left unfulfilled as the production company rejected her request.

In the first *Harry Potter* novel, readers learn that Hagrid is allergic to cats. He sneezes whenever the velvet-pawed animals come near him.

Short & Sweet

Since 2007, you can use Potter postage to send your mail in France, Australia, Great Britain, and Taiwan.

Some names found in *Harry Potter* are relatively rare to encounter in real life. Who would've thought that Ginny Weasley's full name is Ginevra?

Dragons, smacks, and numerous charms – the flying brooms in *Harry Potter* had to endure a lot. That is why extraordinary titanium brooms were used on set.

Rupert Grint put on a rather unique performance to apply for the role of Ron Weasley. He (obviously successfully) applied with a rap video.

Wizard's Chess

Ron uses an impossible move while playing a match of Wizard's Chess against Harry in *Harry Potter and the Sorcerer's Stone*. The piece is supposed to move forward. This move is impossible for a knight – at least in the Muggle world.

The Four Marauders

The Marauder's Map was created by four friends. They inscribed themselves on the map in the following order: Moony (Remus Lupin), Wormtail (Peter Pettigrew), Padfoot (Sirius Black) and Prongs (James Potter). The marauders died in the reversed order as is inscribed on the map.

Mirror, Mirror on the Wall

Most Potter fans already know the Mirror of Erised got his name by reading the word "desire" backward. However, not only does the title have a deeper meaning but even the inscription on the mirror's frame tells something about its purpose. The words, initially unreadable, can be read backward: "I show not your face but your heart's desire."

Short & Sweet

To perfectly depict the Weasleys' flying car in *Harry Potter and the Chamber of Secrets*, there were sixteen Ford Anglias on set. They were all customized in different ways to add their magical qualities to the movies.

Most young witches and wizards are taught magic at home before starting their education at Hogwarts. They don't have enough control over their powers in their younger years to go to a Muggle school.

After Harry dies and the Horcrux inside of him is destroyed, Harry loses the ability to speak Parseltongue.

The place in which J. K. Rowling first got the idea for *Harry Potter* was very fitting: on a train ride to London.

Forest Field Trip

The Forbidden Forest is one of the scariest places in the *Harry Potter* universe – but you can also visit it in real life. The Black Park in Buckinghamshire was the first shooting location for the Dark Forest. Later on, the forest was recreated artificially. This was a massive effort, considering that there were trees with a diameter of over fifteen feet. It was also important to consider that a Ford Anglia still needed to fit through them when arranging the trees.

Names with a Purpose

Some names have the purpose of giving a certain kind of feeling when read. The dementors, for example, are creatures who suck all the happiness from their victims. So instead of something like "bunny buns," their name should be kind of intimidating. The Turkish version is even more accurate, naming them for the things they do. The creature there is known as "ruh emici," which can be translated to "soul sucker."

Short & Sweet

Fans of the movies first learned about Dumbledore's connection to Gellert Grindelwald during *Fantastic Beasts and Where to Find Them*. Readers of the novels learn about Dumbledore's past and his short affair with the Dark Arts earlier.

The destruction of the Burrow – the house of the Weasley family – is a sad scene in the movie *Harry Potter and the Half-Blood Prince* that never occurred in the book.

Hermione wears a blue dress to the Yule Ball in the book *Harry Potter and the Goblet of Fire*. The film producers decided to go with a pink one instead.

Ron Weasley's magical adventure almost came to an early end. J. K. Rowling originally wanted to kill off Harry's best friend in the middle of the story.

An Actress on Her Best Behavior

Emma Watson was also referred to as "One-Take-Watson" or "One-Take-Emma" on set. It is unclear whether she got that name by motivating her co-workers to get their scenes perfect on the first try or by nailing her own scenes instantly. She also might've earned that nickname because her first take always seemed to be the best one.

Boarding School-Phobia

The role of the professor for the elective course Divination was initially meant to be taken on by actress Tilda Swinton, but two things kept her from it. First off, she didn't have enough time for the role because she was working on other projects. Secondly, she had a strong dislike for boarding schools. Because Hogwarts is a boarding school for witches and wizards, she didn't want to play a professor there.

Loyal 'til the End

Alan Rickman stayed loyal to the role of Snape. Because he was the only one on set who knew Snape's true intentions, he opposed the director's instructions from time to time. If Snape was to do something that the actor knew would be uncharacteristic for his role, he made his opinion clear. He refused to do certain things because he, unlike the others, knew what would happen at the end. He never revealed his background to anyone, though – not until everyone was officially privy to it.

Harry Potter Bewitches Laws

Warner Bros.' shooting in the United Kingdom was only made possible by two higher-ups in the British film industry. The company offered to help secure filming locations, provided its Leavesden Film Studios to be used for filming, and made changes to laws regarding child labor in the United Kingdom to allow the young actors to spend some more time in front of the camera.

Short & Sweet

Hogwarts is hidden between several different charms to avoid being discovered. If a Muggle were to stumble upon the exact location of Hogwarts, all they would see is an old ruin instead of a castle.

Even witches and wizards without funds won't miss out on their education. The cost to attend Hogwarts doesn't have to be paid by students; it can be funded by the Ministry of Magic instead.

The Adventures of Harry Potter being translated into Old Greek results in the longest text written in that language in over 1,500 years.

A Dark Premonition

Many symbols and hints of myths find their place in *Harry Potter*. Lord Voldemort's wand also has a deeper meaning. It is made up of yew, which is a symbol of immortality but is also known as a bad omen.

Ignorance Is Not an Excuse!

The scriptwriters unknowingly wrote a mistake into the script for *Harry Potter and the Half-Blood Prince*. The problem was found by J. K. Rowling, who explained the error to those responsible: In one scene, the scriptwriters had Dumbledore talking about a woman he had loved when he was younger. This was impossible, though, as the Hogwarts headmaster is attracted to men. The crew was unaware of that.

Mailings in a Class of Their Own

If you were wondering why you didn't receive a letter to Hogwarts on your eleventh birthday, the letter isn't actually supposed to arrive on one's exact birthday. Aspiring Hogwarts students receive the letter during the summer holidays before the start of the school year. Harry was showered with such letters before his birthday, but his uncle kept him from opening them. Only on his birthday was he finally picked up by Hagrid.

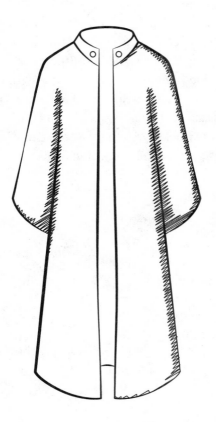

Spoiled by the Simpsons

Famous personalities or events often appear in episodes of the TV series *The Simpsons* – with *Harry Potter* being one of them. In the episode *The Bob Next Door*, Sideshow Bob spoils an important event from the sixth *Harry Potter* novel – Dumbledore's killing by Snape.

Larry or Harry?

When a novel or a book series finds great success, there's one thing you can expect: accusations of plagiarism. The American author Nancy Stouffer is convinced that Rowling copied her work. Larry Potter, complete with glasses and black hair, is supposed to have existed before Harry. Words such as "Muggle" and "Nimbus" also appear in the books written by Nancy Stouffer. Rowling claims these similarities are coincidence.

Harry Potter and the Sorcerer's Stone and *Harry Potter and the Chamber of Secrets* have additional scenes never shown in cinemas. They appeared years later as extended versions of the films.

The 2-in-1-Writer

Mysterious, dark, and creepy are some words that can especially be used to describe the last few *Potter* books. But they could also refer to the thrillers written by Robert Galbraith. You're wondering how that is related to *Harry Potter*? Robert Galbraith is J. K. Rowling. The author used the pseudonym to ensure that her fame didn't affect sales numbers. Rowling wanted to be judged based on her work independent from her already existing success.

Hidden Meaning

Names in *Harry Potter* often have a deeper meaning than you might realize at first glance. "Dumbledore" not only sounds impressive, but it is also an Old English word for "bumblebee." A fitting name for the headmaster that J. K. Rowling always imagined humming while pacing through Hogwarts. The constant humming reminded her of the fluffy insect with stripes.

Short & Sweet

International Harry Potter Day
is celebrated on May 2 of every year.
It is also the day, the Battle of Hogwarts
took place.

Draco Malfoy with a lightning scar and
glasses? Or maybe with red hair and
freckles instead? That mental image isn't
as far-fetched considering that Malfoy's
actor Tom Felton originally auditioned for
the roles of Harry Potter and Ron Weasley.

Countless books can be seen inside
Dumbledore's office in the *Harry Potter*
movies. Most of those books are actually
telephone books with a new cover.

Even though the Catholic Church isn't a big
fan of the Potter movies, the sixth movie,
Harry Potter and the Half-Blood Prince,
received the Vatican's blessing since it
clearly depicted that good should triumph
over evil.

Playing on Repeat

Harry Potter is known for breaking numerous records, and it didn't stop when it came to radios. The wizard from England was the star of the longest-running radio show of all time on Christmas Day 2000. BBC4 broadcasted eight hours of an uncut version of *Harry Potter and the Sorcerer's Stone* without interruptions by news or other regular broadcasts.

Voldemort's Right Hand

The title of "right hand" was often used in old times to refer to one's closest and most loyal advisor. Lord Voldemort never bestows the honor of this title upon anyone officially. Still, it is noteworthy that Bellatrix Lestrange can be seen to Voldemort's right in every scene. Her loyalty and devotion to the Dark Lord are also apparent in the movies.

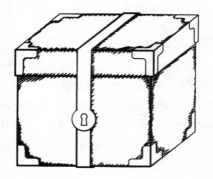

Fight for What Is Good

A fight scene in the eighth movie of the *Harry Potter* franchise in which Professor McGonagall faces off against Snape was supposed to happen without the head of Gryffindor. According to the script, a duel between Harry and Snape was supposed to occur. However, J. K. Rowling insisted that McGonagall get her shining moment by playing an active role in the fight.

Only Coworkers or Something More?

After a few years of friendship, Ron Weasley and Hermione Granger finally become a couple. There might have been some real-life chemistry on set as well. It seems that was only one-sided, though. Rupert Grint (Ron Weasley) and Daniel Radcliffe (Harry Potter) are rumored to have had their eyes on their colleague Emma Watson (Hermione Granger).

Short & Sweet

The design of the Three Broomsticks Inn
was created for the *Harry Potter*
theme park, *The Wizarding World of
Harry Potter.* An exact copy was made later
for the movies.

Before his breakout role as Harry Potter,
Daniel Radcliffe played the role of a young
Copperfield in the movie *David Copperfield.*

J. K. Rowling's parents first met at King's
Cross train station. Whether or not that's
the reason why the Hogwarts Express
departs there is unclear, though.

The Black Sisters

Helena Bonham Carter and Helen McCroy have more things in common than just their names. Both were meant to play the role of Bellatrix Lestrange. The part was passed on to Helena Bonham Carter when Helen McCroy got pregnant. McCroy still has a connection to the role: She later played Draco Malfoy's mother, Narcissa Malfoy, a born Black and Bellatrix's sister.

Choice of Partner Requires Careful Consideration

Readers of *Harry Potter*, *Game of Thrones*, or *Lord of the Rings* make better romantic partners. This conclusion was drawn through a study conducted by the University of Oklahoma. Over 400 people were asked about their favorite genre to give insight into their opinion about gender roles and relationship problems. The study concluded that participants who preferred science-fiction and fantasy genres had a healthier attitude on how a good relationship works. They also tended to have less unrealistic relationship expectations.

Playing with Fire

Sometimes special effects have to be used to help those who can't do magic, but not all effects in the *Harry Potter* movies are animated. The dragon from *Harry Potter and the Goblet of Fire* spits real fire, for example. A flame-thrower with a range of around 40 feet was manufactured for this specific purpose.

A Change Just Like Magic

Anyone who's paid close attention to the movies will have noticed that Harry's wand changes throughout time. While the wizard carries a smooth, even wand in the first two movies, it turns into a trunk-like wand with a more natural and mysterious feel in the third movie. The reason for that is director Alfonso Cuarón; he offered a selection of new wands to the actors before shooting *Harry Potter and the Prisoner of Azkaban*. They were supposed to highlight the individual characters better. An optical change could also happen within the wizarding world. As wandmaker Garrick Ollivander explained, wands can learn from their owners and adjust to them.

Short & Sweet

A truck carrying over 8,000 copies of *Harry Potter and the Order of the Phoenix* vanished from a warehouse in Manchester shortly before the launch of the fifth *Potter* novel. According to experts, the novels had an inestimable worth on the black market.

According to J. K. Rowling, there are approximately 3,000 witches and wizards in the United Kingdom.

If Lucius Malfoy had gotten his way, his son Draco would've almost gone to the wizarding school Durmstrang. He only attended Hogwarts because his mother, Narcissa, wanted to keep him close.

Short & Sweet

Actress Katie Leung (also known as Cho Chang) listened to *Coldplay* in her dressing room to be able to cry more convincingly in her scenes.

One of J. K. Rowling's best ideas came to her while she was on a plane. She used a sick bag to capture her flash of inspiration: Gryffindor, Hufflepuff, Ravenclaw and Slytherin – the names of the four Hogwarts houses.

Hogwarts holds not only exclusive courses and professors in store but also offers luxurious school uniforms. The costumes not only look good, but they're also high-quality: ties made of silk and sweaters made from wool.

Flying Frogs

In the movie *Harry Potter and the Sorcerer's Stone*, on Harry's first train ride – on the Hogwarts Express, to be exact – a chocolate frog leaps out of the compartment's window. As the children of Harry, Ron and Hermione go on their train ride in the last Potter movie, a small chocolate frog jumps into their compartment – coming full circle.

Tiny Elf, Big Help

Even though he was a very popular character, house-elf Dobby only appeared in two of the eight movies – the first time in *Harry Potter and the Chamber of Secrets* and the second and last time in *Harry Potter and the Deathly Hallows – Part 1*. But in the books, the elf has many more appearances and often proves to be a big help. While in the novels, Dobby is the one who tells Harry about the Gillyweed to help him with the second Triwizard Tournament task, in the movies, it's Neville who gives Harry the helpful tip.

Magical Digits

Entering the number 6-2-4-4-2 in a phone booth sends Arthur Weasley and Harry to the Ministry of Magic. On a keypad with the T9 function, these digits would create the word "magic" – a truly magical number.

French Peculiarities

The French have always struggled with adapting terms from other languages. They even changed the full title of *Harry Potter and the Sorcerer's Stone*. In France, it is called *Harry Potter à l'école des sorciers*, which means something like *Harry Potter at the School of Wizards*.

A Gaze at the Future

While watching the second Potter movie, *Harry Potter and the Chamber of Secrets*, viewers can spot little details that go by unnoticed very quickly, such as when Harry and Hagrid walk by a bookstore at Knockturn Alley, where *Harry Potter* books by J. K. Rowling can be spotted in the window. Theoretically, Harry could have read about his future by buying one of those books.

Rulebreaker

Strictly speaking, it is forbidden for underaged witches and wizards to use magic outside of school. The movies didn't always confine themselves to this rule, though. Of all people, top student Hermione breaks the rule twice to repair Harry's glasses. The first time she uses a charm outside of school is inside the Hogwarts Express on the way to Hogwarts in *Harry Potter and the Sorcerer's Stone*. The second time she fixes Harry's glasses is in Diagon Alley in *Harry Potter and the Chamber of Secrets*.

Lineage

Harry and Voldemort are related. The family relations go back to the three brothers to whom the Deathly Hallows were gifted. Cadmus Peverell passed down the Stone of Resurrection for generations until Marvolo Gaunt, Tom Riddle's grandfather, gave it to Voldemort. On the other hand, the Cloak of Invisibility was passed down in the Potter family by Cadmus' brother Ignotus Peverell. That means that the Riddle and Potter families stem from the same bloodline. Another ancestor of Voldemort is Salazar Slytherin, which makes Harry a distant relative to one of the Hogwarts founders.

Laughter Forbidden!

Many jokes and laughs were undoubtedly shared on the set of *Harry Potter*. But when it comes to work, Emma Watson is a true professional. She prohibited Rupert Grint from entering the film set because he couldn't stop laughing during Harry and Hermione's kiss scene in *Harry Potter and the Deathly Hallows – Part 1*.

A Train Crash of a Different Kind

The Hogwarts Express is one of the most popular objects from *Harry Potter*. Sadly, not everyone sees eye to eye on that matter. During the shooting of the second and third movies, the train was vandalized. It was sprayed with green and silver paint at night, which caused around 3,000 British pounds worth of damage. The culprits must have been Slytherin fans, judging by the colors.

Short & Sweet

Phoenixes don't exist in real life.
Someone should've told Lucius Malfoy's
actor Jason Isaacs. Fawkes, the phoenix,
seemed so lively to him that he thought it
was a real bird.

Neville's actor Matthew Lewis had a
favorite quote by his character:
"Why is it always me?"

At the time of the shooting for *Harry Potter
and the Chamber of Secrets*, neither the
audience nor the movie producers knew
how important it was that Harry destroyed
Tom Riddle's diary with the tooth of a
basilisk. J. K. Rowling hadn't revealed
anything about the Horcruxes and their
characteristics at that point.

Suburban Living at a Special Price

All Harry ever wanted was to escape the Dursleys' home, but it seems like the house where the scenes were shot isn't very popular in real life either. The Dursleys' homeowner, Sandra Smith, wanted to sell the suburban house seen in *Harry Potter and the Sorcerer's Stone* for around 480,000 dollars – but nobody wanted to pay that much. The highest bid only offered 430,000 dollars and came from a bidder who didn't even know *Harry Potter*.

A Chair on the Run

In *Harry Potter and the Goblet of Fire*, Dumbledore tries convincing the former teacher, Professor Slughorn, to take up his post at Hogwarts again. However, upon visiting, he finds the professor's house in shambles without any trace of Slughorn. At least it may seem like it until Dumbledore notices a specific chair. How does he realize the chair is actually his old acquaintance? The chair has feet, revealing Professor Slughorn's identity if you pay close attention during the scene.

Short & Sweet

The casting calls for *Harry Potter* roles of all sorts regularly attracted masses of people. When the casting for Luna Lovegood started, the queue stretched out over several streets and even a few blocks.

Dolores Umbridge's Patronus takes the form of a cat.

Quidditch has arrived in the Muggle world. There are several teams and even a Quidditch World Championship in which players with plastic tubes between their legs (as a substitute for the brooms) to try to score points.

Back to the Wild

As The Keeper of Keys and Grounds of Hogwarts, Rubeus Hagrid has spent years raising magical creatures of all kinds. A few were even trusted to carry out special tasks, such as Fluffy, the three-headed dog from the first *Potter* movie. He was supposed to watch over the path to the Sorcerer's Stone and did just that – although not very successfully. If you've ever wondered what happened to Fluffy after the movie's events, then J. K. Rowling revealed he is back in Greece. After the drama around the magical stone, Dumbledore asked Hagrid to release some of his creatures back into the wild.

Authors among Themselves

A lot of background information around the world of *Harry Potter* was only released by J. K. Rowling at a later point in time. To ensure the best portrayal in the movies, Rowling played a part in writing the scripts. Through this, she filled scriptwriter Steve Kloves in on her secrets and details of the *Harry Potter* world. This was the only way to make sure that the development of different characters was portrayed in a convincing matter.

Harry Potter against Coronavirus

The coronavirus pandemic was especially challenging for parents because their children could only attend school rarely or not at all. To offer them some relief and give children a way to cure their boredom, J. K. Rowling created the website *Harry Potter At Home*. On the website, children can take quizzes, solve riddles, watch craft videos and read funny articles – obviously all around the world of *Harry Potter*. Even a few celebrities supported the program, including Daniel Radcliffe. He started out by reading aloud the first chapter of *Harry Potter and the Sorcerer's Stone* in a video. Similarly, the rest of the novel was continued by other stars for several weeks.

Tom Riddle, Child Prodigy

The Dark Lord is one of the most powerful wizards in the entire *Harry Potter* universe. If he didn't turn to the Dark Arts, he could've done a lot of good. After all, he was a child prodigy that created a Horcrux at the mere age of sixteen. Unfortunately, it was wasted potential.

Children's Best Seller

The hype about the *Harry Potter* books hit the whole world. So many copies had been sold even before the fourth book's release that *The New York Times* decided to take a step in a new direction. The newspaper announced the creation of a separate children's best sellers list. The *Potter* books had occupied the general best sellers list for approximately 80 straight weeks.

A Classroom Just Like in Hogwarts

A teacher spontaneously transformed his classroom into a *Harry Potter* paradise – that's how it happened in Hillsboro, Oregon. The teacher, Kyle Huber, decided to pack all of his *Harry Potter* equipment and unpack it inside his classroom – to the enjoyment of his students. They didn't expect any of it and were pretty overwhelmed by the transformation, but it was obviously a positive surprise. The crests of the Hogwarts houses and props like the Sorting Hat or the Pensieve were spread out across the room. The teacher paid close attention to detail and created a classroom that nobody would forget anytime soon.

J. K. Rowling lived and worked in Portugal as an English teacher. That is where she got the idea for the cloaks that the Hogwarts students wear.

They are inspired by the clothing of Portuguese university students.

Forever Young

The death of Severus Snape left many fans heartbroken. The fact that he died so young only made matters worse. Snape was born January 9, 1960, and died on the May 2, 1998, so he was only 38 years old at the time of his death.

Teeth to Take Home

The main characters are not the only ones who appreciated a nice prop to take home. Helena Bonham Carter (a.k.a. Bellatrix Lestrange), too, wanted to take a little reminder from the set. However, her choice was a little different than one would imagine. She chose the faux teeth she wore while filming.

Cuddled Up

Ginny Weasley's actress Bonnie Wright had to lay on the Chamber of Secrets' floor for a prolonged time for a scene in the second movie. The floor was so cold, though, that she put bottles with hot water under her clothing to keep warm.

The School Within the School

The actors were still very young on the film set for *Harry Potter and the Sorcerer's Stone*. Aside from their education at Hogwarts, they also had to focus on their studies in the Muggle world. For that reason, a school was established on set, and Daniel Radcliffe and his colleagues could switch between their Muggle school and Hogwarts without having to miss out on anything.

Picky Casting

In addition to Daniel Radcliffe, the American actor Liam Aiken and the British actor Gabriel Thomson were in the running for the role of Harry Potter. Even though Aiken and Thomson did well in front of the camera, Radcliffe came out on top. However, the reasons that worked against the other two actors weren't very solid. Understandably, Gabriel Thomson wasn't chosen because he was too old for the role, but the only thing that spoke against Liam Aiken was his American origin.

Short & Sweet

In the movie *Harry Potter and the Prisoner of Azkaban*, a wizard reading Stephen Hawking's *A Brief History of Time* can be spotted inside the Leaky Cauldron.

Viktor Krum's actor Stanislav Ianevski needed to learn only two lines and about twenty words for his role in *Harry Potter and the Goblet of Fire*. He didn't say more than this throughout the entire movie.

Emma Watson's natural hair color is dark blonde. She had to dye her hair brown for her role as Hermione Granger.

In Japan, the charms core class is called "Fairy Magic".

Special Seats for Potter Fans

Only two months after the theme park *Wizarding World of Harry Potter* opened its gates in Florida, there were so many complaints that something had to be changed. Visitors were complaining about the size of a rollercoaster's seats. Guests with a bigger girth had to be sent away because the security belt couldn't be adequately closed around them. After many complaints, the park decided to adjust some of the seats. That way, visitors can try out a test seat to see if they need to enter a special queue for the extra seats.

7 x 1 = 95?

In *Harry Potter and the Deathly Hallows – Part 1*, Harry has to flee from Privet Drive. Because the Death Eaters are on his tail, he needs to throw them off; the only option are several Harrys. That isn't a problem, thanks to the Polyjuice Potion, as there are seven identical Harrys. However, there's only one Daniel Radcliffe – meaning the actor had to play each of his doubles himself. Over 95 takes were needed to capture the scenes.

Magic at Home

If you've ever wanted to attend Professor Flitwick's Charms class and try new spells, the PlayStation 3 game *Book of Spells* is perfect. J. K. Rowling and *Warner Bros.* helped develop the game, based on the magical world of *Harry Potter.* You step into the shoes of a Hogwarts student – of course, only after choosing the fitting Hogwarts house and a wand – to learn the art of charms. Thanks to augmented reality, players can use their controller as a wand. The predefined motions need to be mimicked to cast a spell.

Film Set for Felines

Dolores Umbridge is one of the most hated movie characters in the franchise. Her love for tiny, fluffy kittens is probably the only good thing about her. Her office is decorated with images of the velvet-pawed animals. Around 40 real cats were brought on set and filmed for the unique wall decoration.

Awkward Situation

In *Harry Potter and the Deathly Hallows*, Draco Malfoy is hugged by Voldemort for the first time. What may seem like an awkward and stiff scene was improvised by Voldemort actor Ralph Fiennes. The confused look that can be seen on the face of Malfoy's actor Tom Felton was authentic.

Summa Cum Laude

Most universities probably don't deal with *Harry Potter*, at least not as a part of their studies. But the wizard is actually a part of the daily schedule at a university in India. A course of study dealing with the law system in the *Harry Potter* universe can be chosen there. The students learn about generally accepted legal principles and be encouraged to try to apply existing laws to unusual situations.

Lego Lord

Harry Potter characters have taken all kinds of shapes. Their fame has resulted in them appearing in other franchises, including *The Lego Batman Movie*. Voldemort appears as a villain in the film.

Flight-Phobia

In the movie *Harry Potter and the Sorcerer's Stone*, top student Hermione does not seem to be a big fan of the first flying lesson. It looks like this distaste persisted in the following movies. Hermione can only be seen flying a broom in the last Potter movie, *Harry Potter and the Deathly Hallows – Part 2*.

A Theater Visit Led by Destiny

Daniel Radcliffe initially didn't want to audition for the role of Harry Potter. He had previous experience in front of the camera but didn't want other roles. His parents were also worried that the fame associated with an acting career might harm the young Radcliffe. By sheer coincidence, David Hayman, the producer of *Harry Potter and the Sorcerer's Stone*, met Radcliffe and his father in a theatre. He asked both of them to reconsider the audition, and it seems to have worked out.

Spells

The world of *Harry Potter* revolves around magic. Especially in the first few parts of the series, the audience learns a lot about new spells and their effects. But some spells are only introduced in the later parts. The most used charms are "Acio" – the spell that can summon items – and "Expecto Patronum" – the charm that can be used to cast a Patronus.

Sales Record

Harry Potter and the Order of the Phoenix sold twenty-one books per second on its first release day. If you had stacked all books sold in the United Kingdom that day, the tower would be twelve times higher than Mount Everest.

A Flowery Future

Despite Lily and Petunia being sisters, they had very different personalities and lives. However, it seems their parents had a hunch when naming them. While lilies are often associated with death, petunias are associated with anger and resentment.

Short & Sweet

The masks that the goblins wear in the movies for *Harry Potter and the Deathly Hallows* took eight months to produce. Each hair was attached to the masks individually.

The Dursley family has worked with Daniel Radcliffe outside of *Harry Potter*. In several stage performances, Daniel Radcliffe stars alongside Richard Griffiths (Vernon Dursley), Harry Melling (Dudley Dursley) and Fiona Shaw (Petunia Dursley).

When the last scene for the movie *Harry Potter and the Deathly Hallows* finished shooting and the director David Yates yelled "Cut!", everyone broke out in tears.

Detectives, Assemble!

Gilderoy Lockhart is a character introduced in the second *Harry Potter* book. He is a professor at Hogwarts and a good-looking man, according to his „Witch Weekly's Most Charming Smile Award". He is also a liar. That he doesn't always tell the truth becomes obvious no later than the end of the second book. However, viewers could become suspicious way earlier, as a blond wig can be spotted at his desk when Harry and Ron visit.

Time Will Tell

Harry's adventures occur in the 1990s. However, the movies were filmed in the 2000s. Most of the time, there is no problem with that time difference. In the *Harry Potter and the Half-Blood Prince* movie adaptation, things are a little different. In one scene, the Millennium Bridge is shown. The problem: The bridge has only been a part of London's architecture since 2000, making it part of the future in the *Potter* movie.

A Movie for the Tale

Readers and viewers come across stories within stories from time to time. *The Tale of Three Brothers* is especially very prominent in the *Harry Potter* series. It was told in the form of animation within the movie. The tale was so famous that it ended up getting its own movie. Students from the New England School of Communications published a short film telling the story in 2014, only after getting permission from *Warner Bros.*, of course. The movie was shown at several film festivals.

Double Ban

The restricted section in the Hogwarts library is usually off-limits to first graders. Nevertheless, Harry sneaks into it in *Harry Potter and the Sorcerer's Stone*. Duke Humfrey's Library at the University of Oxford was used to shoot the scene. The strict condition that no open flames could be ignited in the library to ensure that the books were protected became a problem. After all, Harry enters the section with a lantern. The centuries-old rule was therefore broken to shoot the movie.

Short & Sweet

According to Hermione, it is essential to hold eye contact while casting a curse to make sure it works.

In comparison to the schools of Muggles, there are very few wizarding schools. That is because a big part of the wizarding community prefers homeschooling.

The shape of a Patronus can change in the event of a strong, emotional occurrence in one's life. After Tonks meets Remus Lupin, her jackrabbit Patronus turns into a wolf – just like Lupin's.

Gilderoy Lockhart has won the "Witch Weekly's Most Charming Smile Award" five times.

Short & Sweet

Draco Malfoy's early supporters, Crabbe and Goyle, appear less and less in the later movies. Jamie Waylett, who acts as Crabbe, was even fired during the seventh movie because he possessed cannabis.
That kind of behavior wasn't tolerable in a children's movie.

Many problems occurred during shooting with young actors on set, one being vocal changes. Radcliffe was so affected by his voice break during shooting that already recorded scenes had to be newly synchronized in post-production.

Harry Potter and the Goblet of Fire is also known as *Harry Potter and the Year without Haircuts* among fans because during shooting, long hair was a popular style for boys.

Historic Witch

There are portraits around Hogwarts of famous wizards and witches from all over the world. Some of them are even famous in the world of muggles – not always a good thing. In the first movie, *Harry Potter and the Sorcerer's Stone*, a portrait of Anne Boleyn can be seen hanging next to the stairs. The former Queen of England was executed, and some believed she was a witch.

When Movies Influence Laws...

...It can only be due to magic. At least the magic around *Harry Potter* and its screen adaptations caused a law to be changed. At the release of *Harry Potter and the Chamber of Secrets* (2002), the movie had a German age rating of six years or older. That was only possible because brutal scenes were removed from the movie. Such wasn't the case in many other countries, which often gave an age rating of twelve. German fans complained about the cut scenes, demanding they be added back. Of course, children still wanted to watch the movie, too. The controversy led to a law change in Germany in 2003. Younger children were allowed to watch movies with an age rating of twelve but with a legal guardian.

Room of Requisites

What happens to requisites used for a movie once shooting ends? Some are kept by actors, while others are donated to a museum or exhibition. Some of them are simply reused. The Room of Requirement, which is shown in *Harry Potter and the Deathly Hallows*, is filled almost exclusively with requisites of the previous *Harry Potter* movies. It accommodates the content of more than 72 containers. Among the props is the chess piece that Rupert Grint (Ron Weasley) sat on during the giant Wizard's Chess match in the first movie.

Breakfast Together

One might think the Muggle world has little in common with the world of wizardry. Now and then, there may be an overlap, which can't be seen as a mere coincidence, such as cornflakes for breakfast. That might not be worth mentioning since everybody must have breakfast. However, when the name of the popular cornflakes are as similar as they are in *Harry Potter and the Goblet of Fire*, there must be a deeper meaning. In the breakfast scenes, movie fans can spot cornflakes labeled "Cheeri-Owls" on the table – a connection to the cornflakes known as "Cheerios" in the Muggle world.

According to
J. K. Rowling,
Professor Dumbledore
is her favorite character
in the *Potter* series.

Wrong Rail

Even though the Hogwarts Express departs from Platform 9 ¾, the scenes were shot between platforms 4 and 5. It all came down to a mistake made by J. K. Rowling. She figured that platforms 9 and 10 were in the part of the train station from which long-distance trains depart. This isn't the case. That is why the shots were filmed at the bigger platforms 4 and 5.

Donald Trump as Voldemort

A *BBC Newsbeat* article questioned why some people refer to the former American president and entrepreneur Donald Trump as Voldemort. The reason for the comparison is Trump's suggestion to forbid Muslims from entering the United States. Author J. K. Rowling commented on Twitter that Voldemort wasn't nearly as evil as Trump.

Short & Sweet

Voldemort has red eyes in the books and in
the first *Potter* movie. Beginning with the
Harry Potter and the Goblet of Fire film,
he is portrayed with blue eyes to seem
more emotional.

The well-known ice cream company
Ben & Jerry's had a limited-time ice cream
flavor called *Berry Potter and the
Container of Secrets.*

Dirk Denoyelle voices Voldemort, Hagrid
and Sirius Black in the Flemish dubs of
the *Harry Potter* movies. Up to the fourth
movie, he was allowed to use
his whispering voice only to record the
voice of Voldemort.

Short & Sweet

One of the rather unusual languages that the *Harry Potter* books were translated into is Low German. The title of the first *Potter* novel in the German dialect is *Harry Potter un de Wunnersteen*, which translates to something like *Harry Potter and the Wonder Stone*.

Booklover J. K. Rowling refused to release the *Harry Potter* novels as e-books for a long time. She finally agreed in 2011, and the first books were released digitally.

J. K. Rowling donated a hand-drawn copy of the Black's family tree to a charity event in February 2006. The drawing was sold for around 30,000 British pounds – to none other than Harry Potter actor Daniel Radcliffe.

Odo the Hero

Aragog, the partly loved, partly hated spider that Hagrid kept as a pet, and almost became Harry and Ron's downfall in the second movie, died in the sixth part of the series. The song that Hagrid and Professor Slughorn sing, while slightly drunk, in the movie *Harry Potter and the Half-Blood Prince* was written by J. K. Rowling. It is called *Odo the Hero*.

No Time for a Breather

The seventh and last book of the *Harry Potter* series was split into two movies. Both parts for *Harry Potter and the Deathly Hallows* were shot like one very long movie – a lot of work for the actors and movie crew. The shooting lasted 236 days.

Magic Wood with Purpose

It is no coincidence that Harry owns a magic wand made from holly. Hermione's vine wood and Ron's ash-stick have deeper meanings as well. J.K. Rowling chose wood types fitting for the character's birthdays according to a Celtic calendar.

Growing up on a Movie Set

The magic trio of actors spent almost their entire youths on *Harry Potter* movie sets. During their last week of shooting, they had to clear out their dressing rooms and take home all of their belongings. This was an especially emotional experience for Rupert Grint: While emptying his room, he found greeting cards he had received for his 14th birthday.

Lost in Translation

House-elves have long been known as little creatures serving wizards and witches. There are, however, free house-elves who are no longer treated as servants. To be free, they must be given a piece of clothing by their master. In Japan, this special status can be a little confusing because "free elves" translates to "free slave-elves." Just to be clear: A free elf is not a slave anymore.

Short & Sweet

The worst thing about shooting the *Harry Potter* movies for Tom Felton, who played Draco, was having to dye his hair light blond. His natural hair color is dark blond.

To sit more comfortably on their brooms, Rupert Grint and Emma Watson, who played Ron and Hermione, let casts of their butts be made. These were attached to the brooms and offered a more comfortable seat.

Shooting for *Harry Potter and the Chamber of Secrets* began three days after shooting for *Harry Potter and the Sorcerer's Stone* concluded. This movie was the only one (except for *Harry Potter and the Deathly Hallows*) produced in the same year as its predecessor.

Old Clothes

The *Harry Potter* movies value authenticity, even across several movies. While Draco Malfoy already makes fun of the Weasley family's lack of wealth in the first movie, the portrayal of the family's poverty can be seen in *Harry Potter and the Chamber of Secrets*. You can also notice the portrayal in Ron's clothing. The difference can be seen very clearly in some scenes: While the other students' cloaks are dyed deep black, Ron's seems somewhat faded and gray. Even the Hogwarts crest looks like it was taken from another piece of clothing and sewed back on.

Potter Maze

The face of Harry Potter's actor Daniel Radcliffe is probably well known to most. But only true fans can see the slight differences in various depictions. A farmer from York, England, takes the cake in this matter. He perpetuated Harry Potter's face in his cornfield. Twice. But you can't only wander through the mazes. Both of the Potter depictions have minor differences. Tom Pearcy, the creator of the masterpiece, wanted to create a huge "Spot the difference" game.

Exploding Teachers

The wizarding community enjoys playing a game called "Exploding Snap." The game is also referred to as "Snape explodes" in the German *Harry Potter* books released before 2008. This title caused readers to associate the game with angry students who wanted to get revenge on Professor Snape. But that isn't the case. The reason for the misunderstanding is the translation from English to German. That's why the game had to be renamed in the German books.

Challenges on Set

The movie crew faced difficult challenges while filming *Harry Potter and the Goblet of Fire.* The second task of the Triwizard Tournament takes place almost entirely underwater. Scenes were filmed in a giant tank with a green background for that purpose. Divers equipped with oxygen tanks were stationed onset to enable the actors to stay underwater as long as possible. Daniel Radcliffe even managed to stay under the water for forty-two minutes.

Preparation Is Everything

Actors do the craziest things to get into their roles. Young actors aren't an exception. Emma Watson, who played Hermione, wanted to embody a top student. That's why she learned her lines and those of her co-stars Rupert Grint (Ron Weasley) and Daniel Radcliffe (Harry Potter). When watching closely, viewers can see her quietly mouthing some of her colleague's lines in *Harry Potter and the Sorcerer's Stone*.

Success in a Bottle

Some details can only be noticed after repeatedly watching a movie. Such is the case in *Harry Potter and the Deathly Hallows - Part 2*. Shortly before the professors cast the protective shield around the castle, Professor Slughorn can be seen drinking a vial of Felix Felicis (Liquid Luck) in the background. A little luck before the big battle can't hurt, after all.

Harry Potter's story starts on a Tuesday, but November 1, 1981, was actually a Sunday.